HOW TO BEAT STRESS

CENTENNIAL BOOKS

M000251999

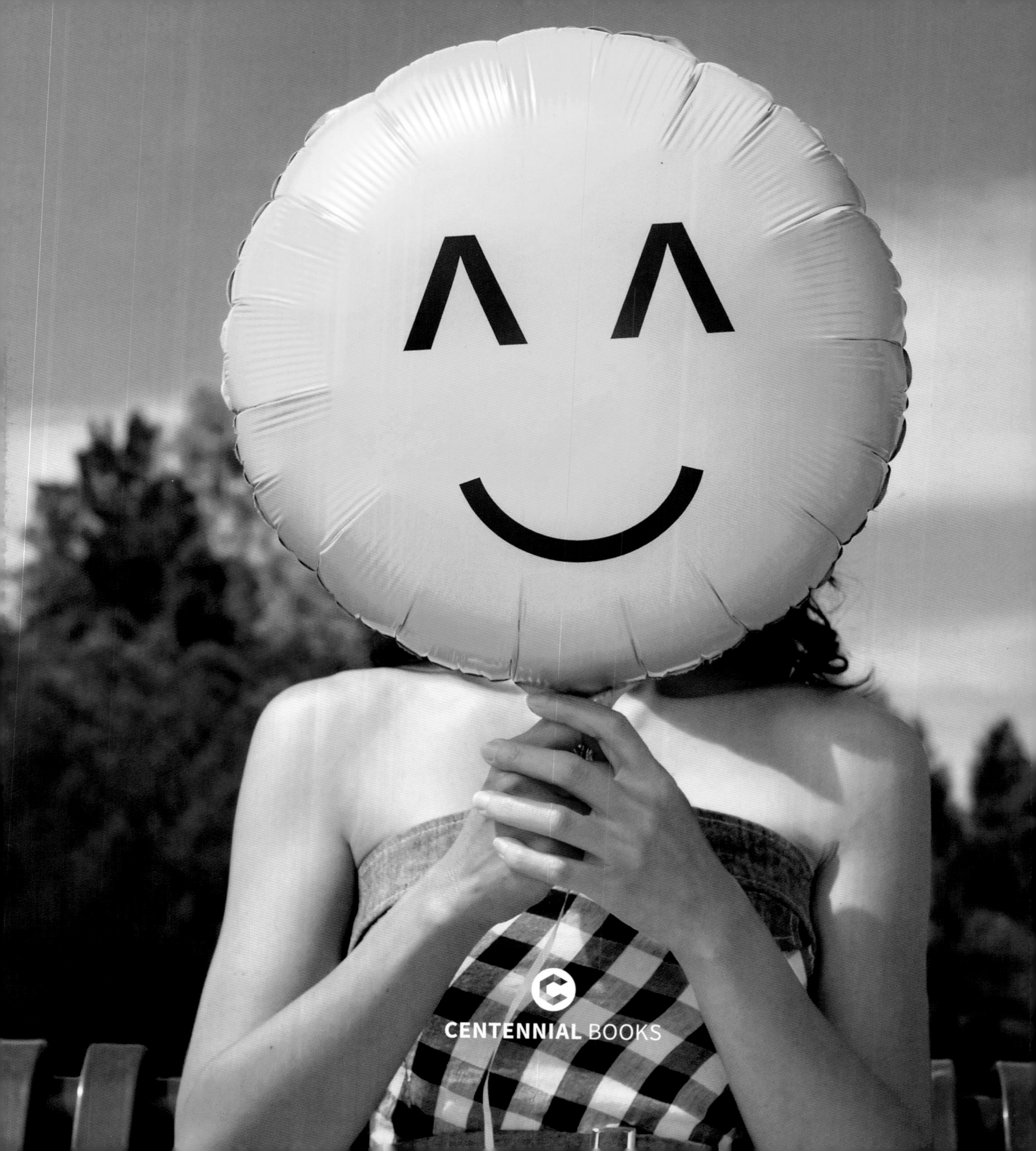

CENTENNIAL BOOKS

HOW TO BEAT STRESS

THE SCIENTIFIC GUIDE TO BEING HAPPY

ALYSSA SHAFFER

CONTENTS

With stress-busting tips, it's easy to look on the bright side.

PART ONE

THE SCIENCE OF STRESS

WHAT DOES INCREASED ANXIETY DO TO OUR BODIES—AND HOW MUCH OF IT CAN WE TAKE? RESEARCHERS ARE JUST BEGINNING TO UNDERSTAND HOW COMPLEX STRESS CAN REALLY BE.

59%

Percentage of
Americans who say
this is the lowest
point in our nation's
history that
they can remember

Little triggers
throughout the day
can add up to major
stress symptoms.

THE STATE OF OUR STRESS

JUST HOW ANXIOUS ARE WE, AS A COUNTRY,
AND WHAT ARE WE DOING ABOUT IT?
RESEARCH SHOWS SOME SURPRISING CAUSES
OF STRESS—AND SOME GOOD NEWS
ABOUT HOW WE ARE STARTING TO HANDLE IT.

here's no doubt about it—we are living in stressful times. There's the day-to-day stress almost all of us face, whether that's balancing work and family or just trying to get from one obligation to the next without spinning out of control. There's technological stress—that endless ping of the phone or stream of social media postings demanding your attention. There's relationship stress, dealing with spouses, or kids, or friends and family. And then there's social concerns, from climate change and politics to gun violence and terrorist threats. With all of these worries, it's surprising we can function at all.

About 8 in 10 Americans say they frequently (44%) or sometimes (35%) encounter stress in their daily lives, according to a 2017 Gallup poll. And the 2018 "Stress in America" survey from the American Psychological Association (APA) found that almost all adults have reported higher levels of stress, with almost half (45%) saying that stress keeps them up at night and 37% reporting unhealthy stress-eating habits.

"People are more likely to report headaches and stomachaches as well as irritability, nervousness and worry, which are signs of coping with chronic stress," says Vaile Wright, Ph.D., director of research and special projects for the APA and a licensed psychologist. Psychologists call this trend habituation—you may not think you're feeling stressed, but your body is still sending off warning signs that all is not well.

WHAT'S STRESSING US OUT?

Your body can't necessarily distinguish where stress is coming from, so whether it's getting stuck in a massive traffic jam or something you saw on the evening news, you may exhibit the same symptoms. Still, experts say there is a wide variety of stress triggers that can affect the way you feel every day.

While personal concerns like work, finances and relationships continue to top the list of stress triggers, the APA notes that social factors can also play a role in our overall stress. "Regardless of where you stand politically, we've found that politics and the current state of our nation are causing people to feel stress," says Wright. The 2017 report noted that across all generations, from the youngest to the oldest, respondents felt that this is the lowest point in our nation's history in terms of how we view our society.

WHO'S THE MOST STRESSED?

The oldest respondents surveyed almost universally seem to have lower levels of stress than the youngest (age 18 and up). One hypothesis, says Wright, is that these older individuals have amassed greater coping skills over the years, so they tend to handle stress better. What once might have bothered you in your early 20s seems a lot less important today. But many of the older individuals are also in less stressful situations—either they retired or work fewer hours, and they don't have young children in the home, so there are fewer day-to-day concerns to worry about.

Younger individuals, on the other hand, worry the most about money. "We know that this is the generation with the highest student loans but who also may not have the caliber of higher-paying jobs that other generations have found," says Wright.

6 in 10

Number of adults who report the current social divisiveness causes them stress when thinking about the nation

MOST COMMON
SOURCES OF OVERALL STRESS

- The future of our nation **63%**
- Money **62%**
- Work **61%**
- Current political climate **57%**
- Violence and crime **51%**

BIGGEST CAUSES
OF STRESS ABOUT THE NATION

- Health care **43%**
- The economy **35%**
- Trust in government **32%**
- Hate crimes **31%**
- Crime **31%**
- International wars and conflicts **30%**
- Terrorist attack in the U.S. **30%**
- High taxes **28%**
- Social security **26%**
- Government controversies **5%**

WHEN TO GET HELP

Not sure if your stress levels have turned from average to alarming? You might want to consider seeing a therapist or other professional if you start to experience the following:

▶ Things that used to make you feel better don't anymore. "If doing something like going for a walk used to help and now it doesn't, or you need to do more of something to get the same response, it might be time to consider why that's not working," suggests Chicago-based psychotherapist Rachel Dubrow, L.C.S.W. You may also start to feel disconnected from things that used to make you happy, like seeing your family or friends.

▶ You just can't stop thinking about what's bothering you, which is known as rumination. These constant thoughts can keep you up at night or start to pervade most every waking moment.

▶ Physical symptoms become more noticeable. Recurrent headaches or stomach pain, constantly getting colds and other illnesses or a low sex drive can be a signal that your stress is getting out of control.

▶ You find yourself falling into unhealthy habits. Whether it's an out-of-control eating binge or a couple of nightly cocktails, you may be trying to manage stress with substances that can take a toll on your health.

▶ Your eating and sleeping habits are disturbed. "If you're eating more than usual—or less—or you're not sleeping, that's a sure sign you may need to get some outside help," says Dubrow.

$300 BILLION

Estimated
cost of stress-
related illnesses
and injuries
in the U.S.
from accidents,
absenteeism,
employee
turnover,
lowered
productivity
and direct
medical,
legal and
insurance costs

Social media and technology also play a significant role. "Millennials are used to constantly being on their devices, and we know from other research that this in itself is a significant factor for stress," she adds.

Women tend to be more stressed out than men, with an average stress level of 5.1 out of 10 for females and 4.4 out of 10 for males. A 2016 study from the U.K.'s University of Cambridge found women experienced stress at nearly twice the level as men. Women often have to carry multiple responsibilities, including juggling work, kids and household duties. Past APA surveys have found that money and work top women's biggest sources of stress, but that family responsibilities now rank third.

Minorities and those who fall lower on the socioeconomic scale are also more likely to report higher levels of stress, with those in the lowest income brackets feeling the most worried. Racial and ethnic minority males also rank their stress levels as being high. These stress levels can lead to significant disparities in both mental and physical health. A 2016 analysis indicated that men whose income is in the top 1 percent live almost 15 years longer than those in the bottom 1 percent. For women, that difference is almost 10 years.

MEN VS. WOMEN

AVERAGE STRESS LEVEL OF MEN:
4.4
(OUT OF 10)

AVERAGE STRESS LEVEL OF WOMEN:
5.1
(OUT OF 10)

Social issues, money and work are among our top sources of stress.

Mindful activities
like yoga and
meditation can
help reduce daily
stress levels.

HOW WE COPE

Despite the high prevalence of stress symptoms, it seems we are taking steps to better manage our response to stress, says psychologist Vaile Wright, Ph.D. "Today more people than ever say they are trying yoga or meditating as a way to manage stress," she notes. Exercise, listening to music and spending time with family and friends are also popular ways to manage stress levels. "It's hard to eliminate stress, but people are becoming better able to cope with it," adds Wright. "It's important to not just feel like a passive victim, but to engage in active attempts to handle stress."

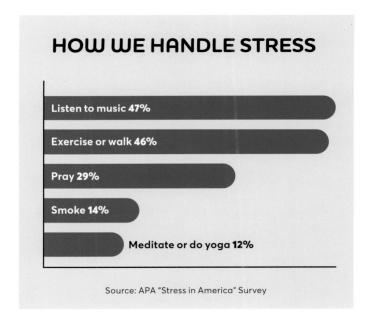

HOW WE HANDLE STRESS

Listen to music 47%

Exercise or walk 46%

Pray 29%

Smoke 14%

Meditate or do yoga 12%

Source: APA "Stress in America" Survey

FINDING SUPPORT

74% of adults feel they have someone they can rely on for emotional support
57% say spending time with family and friends helps them to manage their stress

TOP 10 MOST STRESSED-OUT STATES

Rankings based on stress levels related to work, money, family and health/safety

1. Louisiana

2. New Mexico

3. West Virginia

4. Mississippi

5. Nevada

6. Arkansas

7. Oklahoma

8. Alabama

9. Kentucky

10. Tennessee

TOP 10 LEAST-STRESSED STATES

1. Minnesota

2. North Dakota

3. Utah

4. Iowa

5. South Dakota

6. Wisconsin

7. Colorado

8. Massachusetts

9. Hawaii

10. Nebraska

Source: *wallethub.com*

"HOW I HANDLE STRESS"

Even the calmest, most Zen among us have to face
anxiety-provoking situations. So what do these spiritual leaders do in the
face of aggravation? Here are some of their stay-sane strategies.

THE ZEN PRIEST

"Stress is in your head but it manifests itself in the body. You always assume a worst-case scenario or an amplification of a problem. But your remedy doesn't have to be fancy or pharmaceutical. Both stillness and motion can break the chain of stress you are feeling. For stillness, it's just a matter of trying to quiet the body in order to quiet the mind by taking some deep breaths. Doing this will bring attention away from the head and into the gut. But taking a walk can also help to clear your mind. You have to do so with intention and let the movement itself quiet your thoughts."

—**Karen Maezen Miller, Zen Buddhist priest and author of** *Paradise in Plain Sight: Lessons from a Zen Garden.*

THE RABBI

"I have learned that by engaging in mindful practices, my reactions to stressful situations have changed. If someone bumps into me when I'm walking down the street, my reaction isn't hard anymore—I just try not to absorb it. I've learned that the things that can cause us to constrict are often those we don't have control over, and we're better off harnessing our energies toward things we can control. It's about leading with your heart, and not with your head—thinking about using emotions like kindness and compassion to guide you. I have buttons that say "Be Kind," and I give out about 10 a day. It's a way to fill myself with positive interactions and to minimize stress and frustration. We've started kindness clubs around the country, and to date we've handed out about 20,000 buttons!"

—**Rabbi Laurie Phillips, founder and director of Beineinu, New York**

THE YOGA INSTRUCTOR

"When I find myself in a stressful situation, I tend to use a mantra. It can be a singular sound, like 'om,' or a few words, like 'I am rooted' or 'I am safe.' That helps to keep my mind in the present rather than project into the future or attach to a memory. Even just counting to 10 a few times can force your attention back to the present moment, so you feel less anxious."

—**Amy Pearce-Hayden, founder of the RajaHatha School of Yoga and coauthor of** *Living the Sutras: A Guide to Yoga Wisdom Beyond the Mat*

Key lesson from spiritual leaders: Don't worry about what you can't control.

Chronic stress
can lead to
numerous
health issues.

YOUR BODY ON STRESS

MANAGING LIFE'S EVERYDAY
UPS AND DOWNS CAN AFFECT YOUR
HEALTH ON ALMOST EVERY LEVEL,
OFTEN WITH LASTING CONSEQUENCES.

Describing how stress feels is pretty easy— it's the knots in your shoulders, the monkey brain that refuses to focus, the migraine that knocks you horizontal for hours. But for something that seems so straightforward, what happens in our bodies when we are stressed is fairly complex. When stress is short-term, our systems return to normal pretty quickly. But long-term, or chronic, stress can wear on the body and potentially lead to a number of serious health consequences.

"Chronic stress may lead to persistent increases in blood pressure or blood sugar," explains Susan Everson-Rose, Ph.D., M.P.H, a professor of medicine at the University of Minnesota. "Stress also affects behaviors, and some may try to 'manage' their stress with unhealthy practices such as consuming excess quantities of alcohol, smoking cigarettes or eating high-fat, high-salt 'comfort' foods. Lastly, stress can affect mental health, increasing symptoms of depression or anxiety, which also can increase risk for heart disease and stroke."

And while your body is well-engineered to handle stress on occasion, when you constantly go on red alert, the aftermath can be dangerous. Here's a look at the damage that may be done throughout your body when it is chronically under stress.

Anatomy of the stress response
STEP 1 The nervous system sounds the alarm.
Stress begins in the brain. Whether you're faced with a car as you cross the street or hitting a patch of turbulence on a plane, your senses send a signal to the amygdala, the part of the brain that processes emotions. It interprets these images, sounds or feelings as danger, and sends a distress signal to the hypothalamus, the area of your brain that acts like a command center to the rest of your body.

The hypothalamus communicates through the autonomic nervous system (which controls the body's involuntary actions such as breathing, heart rate, and airway and blood vessel dilation or constriction) that something is awry. The autonomic system itself consists of two parts. Both are always active, although one tends to dominate at any given time. The parasympathetic nervous system is referred to as the "rest and digest" center because it controls the functions that happen at rest and which help us relax. The sympathetic nervous system is the one that takes over when we are stressed. It triggers our "fight or flight" response to stress, setting off a cascade of effects in the body in order to prepare us to face that stress head-on or flee as fast as we can from it.

STEP 2 The troops are activated.
When the sympathetic nervous system gets the alert, it signals the pea-sized pituitary gland in the base of the brain to then stimulate the adrenal glands above our kidneys to produce cortisol and adrenaline (also called epinephrine), which are released into the bloodstream. These stress hormones kick-start other changes in the body to prime you for action, including the following.
▶ **Your heart rate speeds up.**
Adrenaline makes your heart beat faster. Vessels dilate to send more blood to the

muscles, heart and vital organs; pulse and blood pressure rise.

▶ **You breathe more quickly.** These processes require more oxygen—so small airways in the lungs widen, allowing your lungs to take in more air. Extra oxygen is then sent to the brain which can help make you more alert.

▶ **Your senses sharpen.** Sight, hearing, and sound are all more hyperaware as you tune in to your environment, looking for ongoing signs of danger.

▶ **Your liver releases stored energy.** Epinephrine signals the liver to produce more glucose, while fats from temporary storage sites in the body are also released. These nutrients are released into the bloodstream so you have maximum energy to act immediately.

STEP 3 **The process continues.**

Once you've gone through the initial adrenaline surge, the hypothalamus kicks a backup stress response into gear, known as the HPA axis (hypothalamus, pituitary gland, adrenal glands). This axis is triggered by hormonal signals such as CRH (corticotropin-releasing hormone), ACTH (adrenocorticotropic hormone) and cortisol to keep that sympathetic nervous system and its corresponding stress response on alert.

STEP 4 **Calm is restored.**

When the perceived source of stress is removed, cortisol levels start to fall and the parasympathetic nervous system puts a brake on the stress response. Heart and breath rate slow and metabolic processes return to their normal levels.

GENDER GAP

While many stress-induced changes occur in all of us, men and women often respond differently to these processes.

WOMEN

▶ Hormonal changes

Stress throws menstruation out of whack. Symptoms of PMS may become severe; periods can be absent, irregular or painful and the length of your cycle may change. Then when menopause approaches, stress may cause symptoms like hot flashes to increase.

▶ Fertility issues

In a study from the University of Louisville, women who reported feeling more stressed were 45 percent less likely to conceive than those who felt less stressed. And in a study from The Ohio State University, women with the highest biomarkers of stress had a two-fold increased risk of infertility.

▶ Mental health

Women also appear to be at greater risk for depression, anxiety and heart problems due to stress, compared to men.

MEN

▶ Hormonal changes

Chronic stress decreases testosterone levels and sperm concentration, and increases the risk of misshapen sperm or sperm with impaired motility. Stress may also cause or worsen erectile dysfunction.

▶ Mental health

According to a 2017 German study published in *Psychoneuroendocrinology*, a boost in cortisol, as caused by stress, increases risk-taking behavior in men but not in women.

Men are more likely to engage in risky behaviors when under stress.

Stress can lead to fertility problems for both men and women.

CONSEQUENCES OF CHRONIC STRESS

Occasional bouts of stress are no big deal—but a constant barrage can create significant consequences for your health. Here's how some of your body's main systems may suffer over time.

2.3x

Increase in risk of type 2 diabetes among those with chronic stress

Circulatory system

Blood vessels and arteries may be damaged. Chronic stress has been shown to increase the risk of hypertension, cardiovascular disease and stroke. In a study of 48,500 stroke patients published in the journal *Stroke* in 2017, people hospitalized or treated in the ER for depression, anxiety, post-traumatic stress disorder or other psychiatric disorders had a 2.6 times greater risk of stroke within the next 360 days.

Respiratory system

Taking a deep, slow breath is hard when you're stressed. And while gasping for air isn't a problem for most people, stress can worsen asthma or symptoms of emphysema. Acute stress may also trigger asthma attacks, and hyperventilation may trigger panic attacks in those prone to them. "Active stress, which you may have some degree of control over—for example, an argument—may increase inflammation and cause asthma symptoms," explains Simon Bacon, Ph.D., co-director of the Montreal Behavioural Medicine Centre. "Passive stress—things you really have no control over, for example, being stuck in a traffic jam—seems to worsen bronchoconstriction, which makes it harder to breathe."

Digestive system

Stress presents itself in various ways in the stomach. You may experience nausea, pain, butterflies or some combination of these. You may even vomit if the stress is overwhelming. But there's more to the picture than these physical symptoms. Remember, the parasympathetic nervous system stimulates digestion, so when the sympathetic nervous system takes the lead because of stress, digestion slows, you secrete fewer digestive juices and your body has a harder time absorbing nutrients from food. This can cause diarrhea, constipation, acid reflux and heartburn. And while stomach ulcers are typically caused by the bacteria *Helicobacter pylori*, stress can worsen symptoms associated with ulcers, such as abdominal burning or pain, bloating, loss of appetite and frequent belching.

In addition, the call for extra energy in the form of glucose can sometimes backfire when it occurs too often. While the body typically can reabsorb extra glucose, chronic stress has been linked to an increased risk of type 2 diabetes in both women and men—perhaps a 2.3-fold increase, according to a study of almost 13,000 Australian women published in *PLoS One* in 2017. "Previously it was

Being happier
means all
systems are
functioning
at their best!

Too much
tension
can cause
muscles to
grow tight.

thought that stress influenced the onset of diabetes indirectly through mechanisms, such as increased fat around the stomach," says study author Melissa Harris, Ph.D. "Our study shows that stress may impact the way glucose is processed. It is thought that stress hormones may directly alter the body's sensitivity to insulin." If you have other risk factors for diabetes, such as a family history or being overweight, your diabetes risk may be even greater.

Nervous system

Both acute and chronic stress have been found to impair memory. "Areas of the brain that are crucial for memory, such as the hippocampus and prefrontal cortex, are highly sensitive to cortisol, which binds to the neurons in these memory structures and slows their functioning," explains Amy Smith, author of a 2016 study in the journal *Science* and a graduate student at Tufts University. "So when stress causes a substantial release of cortisol, our ability to remember information that we previously knew is often impaired. If this process is repeated again and again, such as with chronic stress, our memory-related brain regions actually shrink in size."

Immune system

In a 2017 study published in the journal *The Lancet*, subjects with higher amygdala activity had higher bone marrow activity, greater arterial inflammation, and a larger risk of heart disease. They also experienced these things sooner than people with lower levels of amygdala activity did. The researchers believe the amygdala may activate bone marrow to produce white blood cells, a key part of our immune system, which in turn causes inflammation and plaque in the arteries, leading to heart attack and stroke.

Researchers also believe that although short-term stress may have boosted our ancestors' immunity, the chronic stress most of us face today is a detriment to our immune system, making us more susceptible to colds and viruses. A new study published in the *Journal of the American Medical Association* also found that stress may increase the risk of autoimmune diseases such as celiac disease, psoriasis and rheumatoid arthritis. "Chronic stress results in immune cells becoming insensitive to cortisol. This interferes with the body's ability to turn off the immune system's production of inflammatory chemicals when no longer needed," explains Sheldon Cohen, Ph.D., professor of psychology at Carnegie Mellon University. This leads to chronic inflammation, which has been linked to an increased risk of autoimmune diseases.

Musculoskeletal System

You've likely heard people say they "hold" their stress in their shoulders or another part of their body. This isn't too far from the truth. Our bodies naturally contract muscles in order to protect us against pain and injury. Studies suggest that stress particularly causes muscles in the arms, neck, shoulders and jaw to tense. Although the tension from long-term stress is not the cause of tension headaches or migraines, it is associated with both. Studies have also found a link between perceived job stress and low back pain, although researchers aren't sure why.

Our bodies naturally contract muscles in order to protect us against pain and injury.

Viewing stress as a positive can make you more resilient.

THE UPSIDE OF STRESS

IT'S NOT ALL BAD. IN FACT, THOSE ANXIOUS EMOTIONS CAN ACTUALLY BE BENEFICIAL WHEN YOU APPROACH THEM THE RIGHT WAY. HERE'S HOW.

The next time traffic makes you late to an important meeting, you could respond the way most of us tend to: Honk, yell at other drivers, tell yourself how you're going to lose this client before they're even a client and otherwise stress out.

Or you could reframe it as positive. You get to finish that podcast you've been itching to hear. Or maybe you call a friend you haven't spoken to in months. Or you could put all that meditation to good use and practice breathwork to remain calm.

Learning to shift your perspective about stress is key, because while we tend to hear that we are overloaded with stress and need to reduce it, stress can actually be a good thing.

"Stress can be debilitating, or it can be enhancing," says Jeremy Jamieson, Ph.D., professor of psychology at the University of Rochester. "Without stress, we would never learn anything, because we need to be in a stressful situation to do things. People who avoid stress don't end up doing a whole lot in their lives."

In fact, learning to welcome, rather than fear, stress can bring you many benefits. "Once you appreciate that stress makes you better and stronger, it changes your brain, it makes you more resilient, and it changes the way you respond to it," says Kathleen Hall, Ph.D., founder and CEO of the Mindful Living Network and The Stress Institute. "Look at CEOs, leaders, people who discover and create things—all of them did not live their lives by avoiding stress; they embraced it."

Here's how stress can be a benefit rather than a detriment, plus how to adopt a

43%

Percentage of highly stressed people who were more likely to die prematurely when they thought that stress was bad for them, according to an eight-year study of more than 30,000 Americans

THE GOOD SIDE OF STRESS

You may never jump for joy about feeling like you're in a pressure cooker, but when your heart begins to race, consider these ways that you're going to be better for it.

1 It may make you more productive.

You're not alone if deadlines tend to whip you into overdrive, causing you to end up doing everything in less time than you thought it would take—and maybe checking a few other things off your to-do list, too. Stress during adolescence has been found to increase productivity in high-threat conditions in adulthood by 43 percent in an animal study published in the journal *Animal Behaviour*. Researchers believe humans who experienced past stress are better able to solve problems when the pressure is on. Over time you may learn to perceive stress as being less negative, or your body may scale back its stress response, explains study author Lauren E. Chaby, Ph.D.

2 It may improve performance.

Acute stress primes your brain to function at its best. In a 2013 study from the University of California, Berkeley, scientists subjected rats to stress, causing their levels of stress hormones to rise. This caused the production of new brain cells in the hippocampus—which plays a role in memory and learning—to double.

Although the rats did no better than a control group on a test two days later, two weeks after the stressful event, they did best their peers. And the researchers found that the new, stress-generated cells were the same ones that helped them shine in the test. It takes two weeks for new

A positive outlook can make you more productive.

neurons in that part of the brain to become functional, the authors noted.

3 It may boost memory.

Some stress may be good for recall, in certain circumstances. According to a 2016 review in the journal *Nature*, "stress facilitates the formation of memory for the stressful event itself and for events that occur less than 30 minutes after," says author Lars Schwabe, Ph.D. "On the other hand, stress may impair the retrieval of unrelated events." Researchers say the release of noradrenaline during stress activates the brain's salience network, which enhances the processing of threat-related information. This may help you remember more details about the stressful situation.

4 It may give you confidence.

Having some stress may give you the confidence to crush your opponents. In a 2015 study published in *Psychoneuroendocrinology*, Swiss researchers first measured the IQs of 229 people and determined their trait anxiety, or how they react to an anxiety-provoking situation. A week later, half the group underwent a stressful situation in the lab,

3 WAYS TO TURN STRESS INTO A POSITIVE

1
Acknowledge the issue: Notice when you are stressed, and what that feels like in your body.

2
Welcome stress. Reaffirm that these sensations are a positive response to a situation that you care about.

3
Use the energy from the stress instead of spending time trying to manage it.

Source: *The Upside of Stress: Why Stress Is Good for You, and How to Get Good at It*, by Kelly McGonigal

HOW TO EMBRACE STRESS

The secret to using stress to your advantage comes in shifting your mind-set to be curious about the stressor and seeking out the positives. Doing so may even lengthen your life: A study in the journal *Health Psychology* found that individuals who reported having a lot of stress and also perceived that stress affected their health had a 43 percent increased risk of premature death. Try these tips to start to welcome stress.

▶ See every obstacle as an opportunity.

"Stress can be enhancing if you see it as an opportunity for growth," says psychologist Jeremy Jamieson, Ph.D. Doing so may also increase positive emotions, heighten your attention to positive stimuli and boost cognitive flexibility, causing you to perform better, he adds.

▶ Notice your body's response.

When you notice your heart thumping, take it as a positive sign. "Your heart beating faster means there's more blood pumping and more oxygen moving in your body. Oxygen helps your brain and organs function," notes Jamieson. Taking a glass-half-full approach like this will help you appreciate how your body acts under pressure.

▶ Find resources.

Ask yourself: Do I have sufficient resources to address the demands of the situation? For example, ask someone for help with a work project. When you feel like you have sufficient resources to tackle the stressor, it will decrease your perception of the stress itself.

▶ Do something.

Stress can spike when we feel we have no control over a situation. Rather than panic, think about one thing you can do to be proactive, says Kathleen Hall, PhD. For example, if the political climate has you worried, write letters to your representatives or donate to charities related to the issues you care about.

▶ Be open to feedback.

Researchers have found that people who have a "stress-is-enhancing" mind-set seek out feedback, even though doing so can trigger stress. That feedback helps you choose behaviors to meet the demands of a stressful situation and value it, as well as set goals to grow, according to the authors of a 2013 study in the *Journal of Personality and Social Psychology*.

then both groups played a game. Compared to the more relaxed control group, those with low anxiety who were stressed were also more confident going into the game. (Those who had higher anxiety, plus stress, were the least confident.) Although researchers are still figuring out why, study author Carmen Sandi, Ph.D., says stress may cause changes in the brain region that controls self-confidence.

5 It may enhance immunity.
While chronic stress appears to make us more susceptible to viruses, acute stress may make our immune system stronger, at least for a little while. Stanford University researchers tracked how immune cells respond to short-term stress. They found that the principle stress hormones (epinephrine, norepinephrine and cortisol) redistribute immune cells, increase the "firepower" of the cells and prime the immune system to function on all cylinders, says study author Firdaus Dhabhar, Ph.D.

6 It fosters resilience.
All of the challenges you face can cause anxiety, but they can also help you learn to deal with other obstacles in life. Research suggests that people who experience a moderate level of adversity during their lifetime develop skills to cope with stress proactively. "Exposure to some stressors—not too many, but not none—promotes psychological toughness," explains Mark Seery, Ph.D., a psychology professor at the University at Buffalo. "The more toughened up people are, the more likely they are to respond well to future stressful things." And you'll come out with fewer bruises than someone with less resilience would.

HOW TO USE ANXIETY TO YOUR ADVANTAGE

No matter the cause of the stress—home, work, politics or anything else—you can find the good in it. Take these three examples:

STRESS MESS **Giving a presentation at work**
NEGATIVE RESPONSE "My heart is racing. I'm going to have a heart attack or pass out in front of everyone."
POSITIVE RESPONSE Remember that your body is priming you to do your best. "This is my body's stress response, and it will help me perform better. My heart beating faster means more oxygen is reaching my brain, so I can think more clearly."

STRESS MESS **Planning a family gathering**
NEGATIVE RESPONSE "This is going to be such a hassle. We can never agree on a date and menu. And then my brother always has to bring up embarrassing childhood stories to make fun of me."
POSITIVE RESPONSE Focus on the fun part of the gathering. "I love watching the kids play with their cousins, and I've been meaning to ask Uncle Joe about Vietnam."

STRESS MESS **Watching the news**
NEGATIVE RESPONSE "I feel powerless."
POSITIVE RESPONSE Take action. Even if it seems small, it will give you a sense of control. "Let me organize a coffee group to talk about these issues on a weekly basis and work together to find ways we can make a difference."

Cravings for sugar kick in when you are under stress.

FOOD FIGHT

DO YOU REACH FOR THE NEAREST BAG OF CHIPS OR
GOOEY BAKED GOODS WHEN YOUR STRESS
LEVELS RISE? TAKE CONTROL OF EMOTIONAL EATING
WITH SOME SIMPLE STRATEGIES.

I am almost a week late on a copy deadline. My car needs yet another expensive repair. My kids are fighting, my husband is going crazy at work and the dog just threw up all over the rug. My reaction? I clean up the mess—then hit the pantry and dive headfirst into a bag of kettle corn.

I'm not the only one to turn to food for comfort when my stress levels start to rise. Nearly 40 percent of adults say they've overeaten or made unhealthy food choices because of stress, according to research from the American Psychological Association (APA). We even joke about it with our friends and post about it on social media. Food, quite simply, makes us feel good, and while stress in the short term can shut down appetite, chronic stress can actually increase our desire to munch—especially on the junky stuff like chips and cookies.

80 percent of people report eating more sweets when they are stressed.

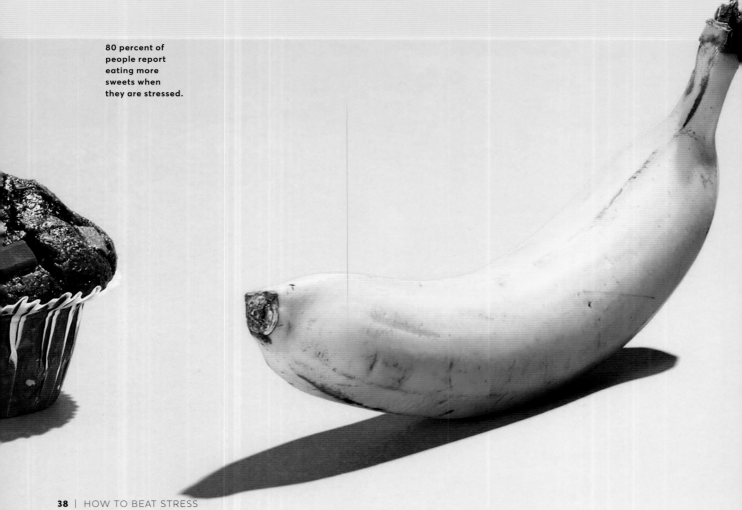

"When stress causes that fight-or-flight mechanism to kick in, the body starts to pump out more of the stress hormone cortisol, which in turn increases appetite and often triggers a desire for food that is especially sugary, salty or fatty," notes Susan Albers, Psy.D., a psychologist at the Cleveland Clinic and the author of *50 Ways to Soothe Yourself Without Food.*

New research also shows that stress affects the part of the brain that monitors self-control, as well as the area that responds to sensory information, like taste. All of that can make a cupcake or pizza look even more tempting, influencing our decision-making and reducing willpower. Then there's the fact that many comfort foods can cause the brain to release serotonin, dopamine and other feel-good, mood-boosting chemicals—at least in the short term.

"Foods that are high in sugar and fat can literally be addicting by down-regulating the area of the brain that serves as the

Research shows that in times of stress, women are more likely than men to turn to food to cope.

rewards center," explains Elizabeth Somer, R.D., a nutritionist based in Salem, Oregon, and the author of *Food and Mood*. At first, she said, you'll get that positive response that helps you feel better almost immediately. "But over time, it takes more and more to get that same sensation—until you're eventually eating not just to feel better, but also not to feel bad."

And then there's the emotional connection many of us have to our favorite foods. "Foods are often loaded with context—they may symbolize comfort from childhood or take us back to a favorite time or place," says Albers. A warm cookie, a big bowl of ice cream and a heaping plate of fried chicken can all take you back to a simpler time.

Of course, the occasional binge on chocolate cake or doughnuts is no big deal. "Almost everyone deals with emotional eating at some point," notes Albers. Even the healthiest eaters have some connection with food and emotions. But it can become a problem when food becomes your only outlet to manage stress, or when it becomes a priority in your life.

"If you find that food is always on your mind when you are feeling stressed, or you notice that you are gaining weight because of your eating habits, you may need to take action to address the amount of stress and your ability to handle it," adds Albers. The benefit of emotional eating is relatively fleeting, she notes. "It's like putting a bandage on a broken arm. You may feel better for a very short time, but it's not going to help you change the situation."

What does help? Try following some of these strategies the next time you get the urge to eat under stress.

Self-medicating can lead to addictive behaviors.

GIVE YOURSELF BETTER OPTIONS

If you have to choose between an orange and some Oreos, it's a pretty good bet you're going to go straight for the package instead of the peel when you're feeling anxious. "Get rid of as much of the junk in your kitchen as you can—if all you have are healthy choices, you're automatically going to make better decisions," notes Somer.

Ultimately this will not only keep you from eating unwanted extra calories, it will also give your body the nutrients it needs to fight stress and keep you healthy. "Sugar, especially, is inflammatory, which can increase some of the damage of chronic stress," adds Somer. "When you make better choices like opting for nutrients such as antioxidants, fiber and healthy fats, you are helping to give your body what it needs to cope and to function at its best."

HIT THE PAUSE BUTTON

If you've ever fired off an angry email only to regret acting out of emotion, you'll appreciate this advice. "We tend to be very reactive to stress, and that can also be the same with food," says Albers. "I try to teach my clients to respond, not just react. Think about your feelings, and how you want to respond in a healthy way." If you've just hung up from an annoying phone call with a friend, don't go straight to the fridge. "Sit down with your feelings for five minutes. Then figure out if you still really want that ice cream—chances are once you've had a chance to process things, it won't be so tempting," Albers says.

Ask yourself why you are eating. Are you really hungry or just snacking because you're anxious? "If you're not truly eating because you are hungry, then drill down and identify the emotions you are feeling," says Albers. She recommends putting together a list of five things you can do when different feelings arise (stress, boredom, anger, fatigue). "This way, you'll have options on hand that will help you address these emotions without having to rely on food." It can be as simple as phoning a friend to vent when you are feeling angry, or doing a crossword puzzle if you're bored.

FOCUS ON YOUR FOOD

Often when we eat out of stress it's less about what we are eating and more about how we are doing it. "With a lot of mindless eating habits, we tend to just sit down and not pay attention to how much we're consuming until we're at the bottom of the bowl," says Albers. Distracted eating (she calls it "zombie eating") means you're not sensing or experiencing your food, so you don't get much pleasure out of eating it.

Instead, make an effort to focus on how and where you are eating. Sit down at a table with your plate and silverware. "Take a moment to be mindful. Put your feet on the floor. Sit up tall and feel your back against the chair, noticing your posture," says Albers. Then, take time to savor each bite, noting how it feels in your mouth and how it tastes. Slowing down your eating and paying attention to your food will ultimately help you enjoy it more. "You can even have whatever it is you are craving—it's ultimately more about eating that food in a mindful way and not going overboard," she adds.

STRESS AND ADDICTION

Food is just one addiction that can form as a response to chronic stress. Research has long identified a link between stress and substance abuse, with acute exposure to stress increasing the escalation of drug use and abuse. "It's common for us to want to self-medicate, and often this will lead to having that extra beer, or two or three, or reaching for a cigarette if you have a history of smoking," notes Rachel Dubrow, LCSW, a therapist based in Chicago.

Most times, our behavior levels return to normal when our stress levels die down. But sometimes chronic stress can lead to an addiction that can require outside help. The National Council on Alcoholism and Drug Dependence (NCADD) identifies these warning signs.

SIGNS OF ALCOHOL DEPENDENCY

Temporary blackouts or memory loss

Recurring arguments or fights with family members or friends; irritability, depression or mood swings

Continuing to use alcohol to relax, cheer up, sleep, deal with problems or feel "normal"

Headaches, anxiety, insomnia, nausea or other unpleasant symptoms when you stop drinking

Flushed skin and broken capillaries on face; husky voice; trembling hands; bloody or black stools or vomiting blood; chronic diarrhea

Drinking alone, in the morning, or in secret

SIGNS OF ADDICTION

Loss of control

Neglecting other activities

Taking risks to obtain drug of choice

Relationship issues

Secrecy (hiding amount of drugs consumed)

Changing appearance; deterioration in hygiene

Increased tolerance (needing more of the substance to produce a reaction)

Withdrawal (anxiety, jumpiness, shakiness or trembling, sweating, nausea, vomiting, insomnia, irritability, fatigue, loss of appetite)

BEST FOODS FOR STRESS EATING

Whether you're craving sweet or salty, turn to these healthier choices when stress cravings strike, says nutritionist Elizabeth Somer.

IF YOU WANT SWEET...
▶ Watermelon, blueberries, mangoes, strawberries, raspberries, blueberries, grapes, bananas or other fruits.

IF YOU WANT CRUNCHY...
▶ Dip baby carrots, pepper slices, broccoli or cauliflower in hummus or another bean dip, or nut butter. Nuts are also a good choice, but be careful not to overdo it, as they can be high in calories. Or bake kale or chickpeas, seasoned with salt and pepper.

IF YOU WANT CREAMY...
▶ Try Greek yogurt and fresh fruit (look for the lower-sugar or unsweetened kind and add a touch of honey or jam), or smoothies made with frozen bananas, berries or other fruit and almond or soy milk.

Have healthy choices on hand for when stress strikes.

SCIENCE OF STRESS

We've all had high-stress moments but how much does it affect your overall health?

STRESS TEST

HOW MUCH DOES STRESS AFFECT
YOUR DAY-TO-DAY LIFE? TAKE THIS QUIZ FROM
MENTAL HEALTH AMERICA—A
LEADING COMMUNITY-BASED NONPROFIT
DEDICATED TO PROMOTING
THE MENTAL HEALTH OF ALL AMERICANS.

1

Do you find yourself "eating emotionally": eating unhealthy foods or eating when you're not hungry, as a response to stress or difficult feelings?

a. No. I eat a healthy diet, and only eat when hungry.

b. I admit I've binged on the occasional Häagen Dazs, but it's not a regular occurrence.

c. Yes. I have to admit that my diet is pretty unhealthy.

2

Are you getting regular exercise?

a. Yes. I lead an active lifestyle and exercise at least three times per week.

b. Sort of. I get some exercise throughout the day, or I go to the gym a couple of times a week.

c. No. I live a sedentary lifestyle and don't go to the gym regularly.

3

Do you find yourself sweating excessively when you're not exercising?

a. No.

b. Sometimes, when I'm particularly stressed, but not often.

c. Yes, it happens fairly regularly.

4

Are you suffering from burnout, anxiety disorders or depression?

a. No.

b. I don't know.

c. Yes.

5

Do you often find yourself with tension headaches?

a. No. I've had them before, but not often.

b. Sort of. I get them once a month or so.

c. Yes. I struggle with them regularly.

6

Are you experiencing any digestive problems, such as indigestion, ulcers or irritable bowel syndrome?

a. No.

b. I get the occasional stress-related stomachache, but nothing too regular.

c. Yes. I'm experiencing pretty regular digestive problems.

7

Are you having trouble maintaining a healthy weight? Or are you carrying excessive abdominal fat?

a. No. I'm within 10 pounds of my "ideal" weight.

b. To a degree. I struggle with diet like many people, but it's not too much of a problem.

c. Yes. I've put on much more weight than I'm comfortable with; I can't keep weight on; and/or my problem area is my abdomen.

52.7%

Number of adults in the U.S. with a mental illness who receive no treatment— that's more than 26 million people, according to Mental Health America

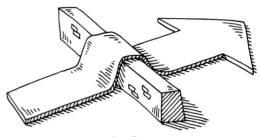

8

Are you easily irritated lately?

a. No. I'm pretty even-tempered. It takes quite a bit to get me flustered.

b. Somewhat. I find I have less patience than I'd like, but it's not a problem.

c. Yes. I find myself snapping at people, or having a low threshold for annoyances.

9

Do you often feel fatigued at the end of a day?

a. Not too much. I'm ready for sleep at night, but I do have energy in the evenings.

b. Somewhat. I come home and need to rest for a while before I can do activities in the evenings.

c. Yes. In fact, I'm often fatigued by the middle of the day.

10

Do you ever have trouble sleeping?

a. Rarely or never.
b. Sometimes I'll have trouble falling asleep, staying asleep or getting quality sleep.
c. Yes, I pretty often have trouble with sleep quality, or with falling and staying asleep.

11

Do you have a supportive social network, and take time for relationships in your life?

a. Yes. My friends and family help with stress.
b. Somewhat. I have a few close relationships and can talk to people if something is bothering me, but don't have as much time for relationships as I'd like.
c. No. I have few close friends or family ties, or I don't have time to devote to the people I could be close with.

12

Are you taking care of yourself?

a. Yes. I take good care of my body and soul.
b. I don't have as much time for self-care as I'd like, but I'm doing OK.
c. No. I rarely take care of myself.

13

How often have you missed work in the last year due to actual illness?

a. Maybe once.
b. Two to three times.
c. Four times or more.

14

Do you have a feeling that stress may be affecting your health?

a. Not really. I'm just taking this test for fun.
b. Possibly. I'm not sure, but I wouldn't be shocked if it were true.
c. Yes. In fact, I'd be surprised if stress weren't affecting my health.

15

Do you find yourself smoking and/or drinking to excess as a way to deal with stress?

a. No.
b. I do one of those things, but it's not a big problem.
c. Yes. To be honest, I know it can't be good for me.

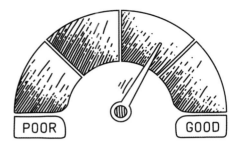

POOR   GOOD

HOW YOU RATE

If you answered mostly a's: You're in good shape!

You appear to have a pretty healthy handle on your stress levels, and are most likely experiencing minimal consequences to your health as a result of stress-related physical responses. Good for you! If you'd like to learn more about how stress could affect your health or the health of those you love, read the rest of this book.

If you answered mostly b's: You could be doing better....

You may be experiencing a degree of stress-related health effects. While you may not be having serious health consequences yet, it's important to lead a healthy lifestyle that includes minimal stress, as stress over time can lead to more serious problems.

If you answered mostly c's: You're in trouble.

You appear to be at high risk of experiencing health consequences due to your stress levels, or you may be experiencing them already. It's vital to manage stress in your lifestyle to safeguard your health or prevent further damage. Read on to learn how stress affects your health and find resources on how to stay healthy.

▶ For more information, check out the Mental Health America website at *mhanational.org*.

PART TWO

CONQUER YOUR BIGGEST CONCERNS

FROM SOLVING MONEY MATTERS
TO MANAGING A HEALTH-CARE CRISIS,
HERE'S HOW TO TAKE CONTROL
OF WHAT'S WORRYING YOU THE MOST.

Americans' debt levels are among the highest ever.

MANAGE YOUR MONEY

ANXIOUS ABOUT YOUR BANK ACCOUNT?
GET A HANDLE ON YOUR FINANCES
AND GAIN CONTROL OVER ONE
OF OUR BIGGEST SOURCES OF STRESS
WITH SOME SIMPLE STRATEGIES.

30%

Percentage of adults in the U.S. who get stressed about saving for retirement

Americans are worried about money. According to the American Psychological Association (APA), about a third of us say unexpected expenses make us anxious; 3 in 10 also get stressed thinking about saving for retirement. And 25 percent are concerned about their ability to pay for essentials like food, clothing and shelter.

Americans' debt hit a new high of $13.86 trillion in 2018, $1.2 trillion higher than the previous peak of $12.68 trillion set in 2008, according to the Federal Reserve Bank of New York. Fewer people say they carry no debt compared to the previous year, with the average personal debt (exclusive of home mortgages) exceeding $38,000, according to Northwestern Mutual.

So it's not surprising that about 65 percent of us report losing sleep over money worries, according to a creditcards.com poll. But with some simple planning, experts say you can gain control of your finances—and reduce those dollar dilemmas.

1 Figure out where your money is going.
Knowing where your dollars are spent is the first step toward being able to take realistic measures to dial things back. "Many of us have no idea what we're spending our money on," notes Tara Murphy, a consumer savings expert and former editor-in-chief of thestreet.com. Start by gathering up all of your bills and credit statements, and begin to break down your spending into various categories, such as meals and entertainment, shopping, groceries, home, etc. You can also begin tracking expenses or use a financial-planning app (check out a few of our favorites, page 57). Keep it up for about a month. "You might be surprised at how much you are actually spending in different areas," says Murphy. That $4 daily latte can actually end up costing you well over $1,000 a year; paying for a cellphone and a landline may be costing you a few hundred dollars more.

2 Set your priorities.
There are some basic rules when it comes to determining where money is going. "Consumer debt, like credit cards, shouldn't exceed 20 percent of your net income [after taxes]," says certified financial planner Marc Lowlicht, CEO of OPES Private Wealth Management in East Hampton, New York. Monthly housing costs (including principal interest, taxes, association fees and homeowners insurance) shouldn't exceed 28 percent of gross income. And your total monthly payments on all debt shouldn't exceed 36 percent of gross monthly income, he advises.

3 Pay down what you can.
Those monthly carrying charges on your credit card are slowly eating away at your finances. The Federal Reserve reported that total credit card balances have increased to $868 billion. The average American has a credit card balance of $6,375, according to credit reporting agency Experian. The average U.S. household pays a total of $1,292 a year in interest charges, according to cnbc.com, which notes that 43 percent of Americans carry a credit card balance for more than two years.

"If you only pay the minimum balance on your credit card, you will never make a dent," says Murphy. That's especially true when interest rates are on the rise. Pay off what you can, and be sure to reach out and talk to your credit card companies if you are having a problem, she adds. "They want to keep your business, so they will try to do what they can to work with you." And don't

Keep a nest egg for any unexpected expenses.

be afraid to transfer balances from your higher-rate cards to your lower-rate ones.

If you have a few different debts, make sure that you pay the minimum on all of them. But it can also help to determine whether you want to pay those with the highest rates first (known as the "avalanche method") in order to pay down the debts that cost you the most in interest,

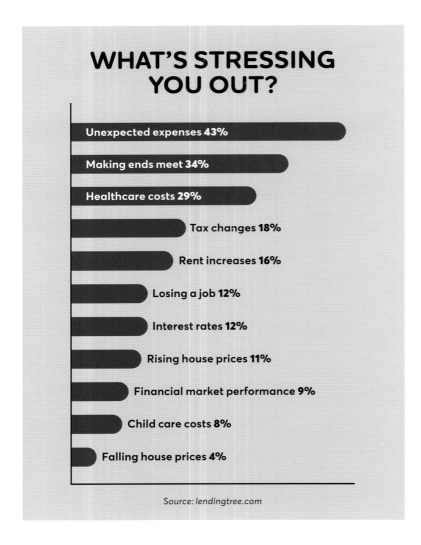

WHAT'S STRESSING YOU OUT?

- Unexpected expenses **43%**
- Making ends meet **34%**
- Healthcare costs **29%**
- Tax changes **18%**
- Rent increases **16%**
- Losing a job **12%**
- Interest rates **12%**
- Rising house prices **11%**
- Financial market performance **9%**
- Child care costs **8%**
- Falling house prices **4%**

Source: lendingtree.com

or if you want to try the "snowball" effect, where you knock out smaller debts before larger ones as a way to gain momentum and to help keep you feeling motivated.

4 Build up your piggy bank.
At the same time that you are trying to get out of the red, do what you can to get more green. Ideally, you'll want to have a nest egg of 6 to 12 months in savings as an emergency fund.

That's something that a lot more Americans need to do. According to the Federal Reserve, 44 percent of us don't have enough funds on hand to cover $400 in expenses; a report from bankrate.com says that 1 in 4 of us don't have enough saved up for major expenses, like big medical bills or a job loss. "Starting out small—even just $50 a month in savings—can help you build up a cushion," says Murphy. "Having that savings goes a long way toward giving you some extra peace of mind."

5 Plan your purchases.
You may really want that brand-new SUV or motorcycle in your garage, but do you actually have a way that you can pay for it? "A lot of our anxiety comes from not being able to keep up with monthly payments—that push-pull that comes from wanting something but also having to find the means to make it work," says Murphy. Thinking about how you will fund big purchases in advance will keep you on track so your financial anxieties don't get out of control. "You can have anything you want, as long as you have a realistic plan to pay for it," adds Murphy. "That alone will alleviate a huge amount of stress."

6 Be careful about consolidation.

If you've gotten into a serious financial hole, you may be tempted to sign up for a debt-settlement program. This is typically offered by for-profit companies, who will negotiate with your creditors on your behalf so you can pay a lump-sum settlement that is less than the full amount you owe. The program will usually ask you to set aside a specific amount of savings each week into an escrow-like account that will help you pay off these settlements. But keep in mind that these programs do carry with them a few risks.

For one, they can adversely impact your credit rating, says Murphy. "If you need to purchase something where credit comes into play, like loans for a car or for school or a home, you may have a problem," she notes.

7 Be a smarter investor.

If your financial plans involve investing in things like the stock market or individual funds, know what you are getting into up front. It can help to sit down with an expert who understands asset allocation and will work with you to create a portfolio that matches your planning, suggests Lowlicht. "People start to panic if the market is down or things aren't going the way they expect, but if you have a plan in place, you'll be able to weather most storms," he shares. Furthermore, be sure to keep updating the plan as your needs change, whether you are getting married, having children or switching jobs. At a minimum, Lowlicht continues, take a look at your investments on an annual basis to make sure that they are in line with your overall needs.

4 APPS TO MANAGE YOUR MONEY

▶ **MINT** Consumer groups consistently love this easy-to-use app from Intuit (creator of TurboTax and QuickBooks) as an all-in-one way to build a budget, track your spending, pay bills and more. You can even use it to get a free credit score, so you know where you stand. *(free)*

▶ **WALLY** Get a 360° view of your finances with this user-friendly app, which allows you to keep track of your expenses and income, scan receipts and set a savings target. The more you use it, the more personalized it gets. You'll even get detailed infographics of data like where you were and who you were with when it comes to how you spent your money. *(free)*

▶ **PRISM** Stay on top of your bills with this simple tracking app, which syncs your account balances and bills in one simple program. Pay bills right from the app (or schedule a payment for later)—it'll send an alert when the money is due and let you know when payment is confirmed. *(free)*

▶ **ACORNS** Turn that spare change into some real dough. With this app, whenever you make a purchase with a card you designate, it rounds up to the next dollar amount and automatically invests that difference in an investment portfolio of low-cost funds that you've preselected based on your risk tolerance. Shop with certain partner brands (like Apple or Nike) and they'll also invest in your account. *($1-$3 a month)*

Spend time
together—and
time apart.

COUPLES COUNSELING

LEARN HOW TO IDENTIFY THE STRESSFUL SPOTS YOU'RE EXPERIENCING TOGETHER AND TAKE STEPS TO OPEN COMMUNICATION SO YOU BOTH FEEL HAPPIER.

Whether you've been dating for a few months or have been married for decades, it's normal for couples to hit a bump in the road. And fighting with your significant other continues to rank among the most common sources of stress today. To smooth things over and get back to a more positive relationship, it's important to be able to recognize when issues come up—and how to approach them. Here, relationships experts explain 10 common sticking points and the best ways to navigate them.

The smallest thing can cause the greatest stress when we don't understand why.

—MELISSA KRECHLER, MIND-SET COACH

1 THE PROBLEM You want things your way.

At some level, we're all creatures of habit—and it can be hard to break out of our regular patterns. So if you are someone who thinks the garbage should be taken out every night but your partner wants to wait until it's full to the brim, a simple request can quickly snowball into a full-on feud. "The smallest things can cause the greatest stress, yet we don't take the time to understand why," notes Melissa Krechler, a mind-set coach who counsels couples and individuals.

FIX IT Take the time to talk to your partner about what's really bugging you. "Explain why you feel the way you do, and see if you can come to some understanding of each other, as well as an arrangement moving forward," says Krechler. You should be able to come up with a solution that both of you can live with.

2 THE PROBLEM Your partner does not like your family.

"This is a common scenario, since your partner likely started dating you because they like you, not because they like your dad," says Raffi Bilek, L.C.S.W.-C., a couples counselor and director of the Baltimore Therapy Center. "And that's OK—your partner doesn't have to like your family members; he or she just has to be nice to them."

FIX IT Be understanding of the position your partner is in—after all, you've been living with your family your whole life. But discuss your feelings about the situation while trying to avoid being defensive. For example, calmly explain to your partner why you don't want him or her to speak derogatorily about your parents. In this way, you can help your significant other start to tolerate some of the difficult behaviors you may have been used to for years, says Bilek.

3 THE PROBLEM You withhold praise for your partner.

Everyone knows the power of positive feedback, and relationships are no different when it comes to wanting validation. Unfortunately, we don't always do the best job of communicating value or praise to our partners. "In the hustle and bustle of life, it's so easy for us to look for what's going wrong while ignoring the things that are going right," says Allen Wagner, L.M.F.T., a licensed marriage and family therapist in Los Angeles who specializes in relationships. "Due to this unfortunate dynamic, many partners find themselves in defensive postures more commonly than they should."

FIX IT Rather than focusing on the negative, make an effort to note what your partner is doing well. "Try to praise your partner daily for something you find makes them irreplaceable," says Wagner.

That can be something as small as the way he makes you coffee in the morning or as significant as how she makes sure the kids always have a healthy lunch. "This can lower these defenses and create a better environment for constructive collaboration," he adds.

4 THE PROBLEM One person takes more than they give.

In every relationship there will be times where one person puts more into the relationship than the other. However, if it goes on for too long without addressing it, it can lead to stress and conflict.

FIX IT Don't be afraid to ask for assistance. "Telling your partner that you would like some help or that you need them to take the responsibility for something—or even to split it—will go a long way," Krechler says. "Also, don't assume that the other person is using you. He or she may not even realize that they are not helping in the ways that you need."

5 THE PROBLEM Your partner made a mistake.

Messing up is human nature. But often, a slipup on one person's part can make the other partner critical or angry. The guilty party becomes defensive, or worse, goes on the attack about the other person's faults, and an argument ensues.

FIX IT "When your partner makes a mistake, the best thing you can do is remember that you're not perfect either and treat them with empathy," Bilek says. "Ask yourself: Could you have made this mistake? Even if your answer is no (you're always on time and they're late again), do you ever make any mistakes? The answer there is probably yes. And if so, how

would you like to be treated when you are the one who messed up? Treat your partner that way and you'll save your relationship a lot of strain."

6 THE PROBLEM You have limited alone time.

"Being in a long-term relationship has many positives, but it is also time-consuming and increases the obligations we have in our lives," Wagner says. "Relationships require a certain level of selflessness that can lead partners to resent one another due to decreased time for hobbies or self-care, less time with friends and increased compromise."

FIX IT Couples often find it hard to assert boundaries for "me time" out of guilt, or fear of disappointing or rejecting their partner, notes Wagner. But this time is essential and can be carved out in healthy ways. So aim for quality time over quantity. Make specific plans together while also opening up your calendar for just you. For example, plan an elaborate date or excursion, or even a vacation, which will build security and safety in the relationship, he advises. This can help your partner feel less jealous or insecure when you are apart. But don't forget to also give yourself time to go on a bike ride, listen to your favorite music or just do what you love.

7 THE PROBLEM You put your relationship last.

Between careers, family, money, kids and friendships, it can be tough to make your partner your priority. But don't let him or her stay on the back burner for too

Research shows that married people are on the whole relatively happy.

**—ED DIENER,
PH.D.,
PSYCHOLOGIST**

Maintaining a
healthy sex life
keeps you more
connected.

long. "There are going to be times where life itself is a struggle," Krechler says. "This is the time to remember that your partner is going through this with you."

FIX IT Make an effort to talk to your partner about what's going on in your life, and keep the lines of communication open. Things getting stressful at work? Be sure to let your partner know how you feel so that he or she doesn't get the impression that something else is coming between the two of you.

8 THE PROBLEM You feel like your partner just isn't "getting" you.

Sometimes it can be hard to get your point across. "It seems like you can never communicate properly with each other—you say something and your partner misinterprets it; he or she makes an offhanded comment and you feel terribly offended," Bilek says.

FIX IT Take a minute to make sure you understand where your partner is coming from. "Listen before talking back, and reflect what you're hearing," notes Bilek. If your partner is angry because of something you did, make sure you understand the problem. Saying something as simple as "it sounds like you're mad because I forgot to get the milk again" can avoid a blowup. "You'd be surprised how often people misunderstand their partner's intention, either because they didn't fully understand their partner's point, or because their partner didn't express exactly what he meant," Bilek says. It's irrelevant whose "fault" it is—more important is using the tools to get on the same page, rather than arguing about who said what when.

9 THE PROBLEM You're more roommates than romantic.

All those nights with Netflix and takeout can start to blend together. Then there's scrolling through your phones together on the couch, talking about the dog-walking schedule for the week and having separate bedtimes. "Many couples can fall into roommate-like territory if they become homebodies and start developing unhealthy patterns," Wagner says. "The end result becomes the absence of sex in the relationship." While there may not be high-level conflicts about this, he adds, it can lead to insecurity around attractiveness, as well as a path toward lower self-esteem and resentment.

FIX IT Both parties usually play a role in the slide toward being more platonic, but it can feel difficult to discuss. Talk about it anyway, says Wagner, and avoid placing blame. Instead, express how you miss sex and the positive ways it made you feel more connected. "Coming from a place of hurt and love rather than anger, resentment or blame will usually lead to a motivation to make each other happy," he adds.

10 THE PROBLEM You have too many expectations.

"We put a lot of expectations on our partners to be, act, live or love a certain way and this is rarely ever going to happen," Krechler says. "When we put these expectations on them, we push them away by making them feel inadequate, unwanted, unworthy and unloved."

FIX IT Before holding your partner to a specific standard, ask if what you would like is in the scope of his or her ability. Seem unreasonable? Dial things back toward what you truly think is acceptable.

TOP RELATIONSHIP STRESS TRIGGERS

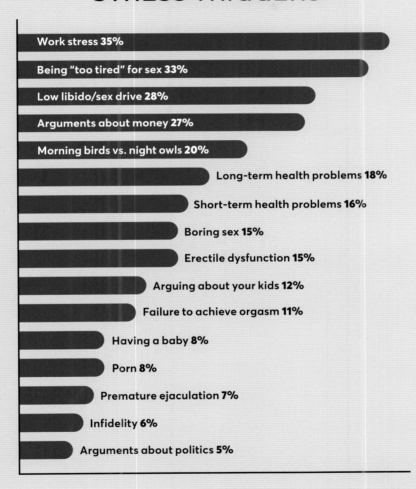

Work stress **35%**

Being "too tired" for sex **33%**

Low libido/sex drive **28%**

Arguments about money **27%**

Morning birds vs. night owls **20%**

Long-term health problems **18%**

Short-term health problems **16%**

Boring sex **15%**

Erectile dysfunction **15%**

Arguing about your kids **12%**

Failure to achieve orgasm **11%**

Having a baby **8%**

Porn **8%**

Premature ejaculation **7%**

Infidelity **6%**

Arguments about politics **5%**

Source: "The Happiness Index: Love and Relationships in America," commissioned by eharmony and conducted by Harris Interactive from 2,084 online interviews of adults age 18+ who are married or in a long-term relationship.

Keep your parents
involved in
big decisions.

STUCK IN THE MIDDLE

HOW TO ADDRESS COMMON SOURCES OF WORRY FOR THE SANDWICH GENERATION.

For many of us, there are the demands of daily life—work, parenting, nurturing a marriage and other important relationships—on one side, and the worry of caring for aging parents on the other. According to the Pew Research Center, 47 percent of adults in their 40s and 50s have a parent aged 65 or older and are either raising a young child or financially supporting a grown child (age 18 or older). Known as the sandwich generation (in the middle, getting squeezed from all sides), it's easy for these adults to feel overwhelmed by their obligations.

"Everywhere you look there is someone tugging at your sleeve. I hear the stress when I talk to people. It's, 'Oh, my goodness, I have a job and kids. Now I have to think about my parents, too?'" notes Joy Loverde, author of *Who Will Take Care of Me When I'm Old?*

Rebekah Aronson experienced this firsthand. Her father had a severe stroke and it fell to her to be there for her parents emotionally and practically, including handling finances and moving them to a new living situation. "Instead of fulfilling my promise of going back to work when [my daughter] was settled into school, life threw major curveballs at us. This is not the life I imagined when I chose to focus on my career back when I was in my 20s and 30s!" Those curveballs may keep coming, but there are ways to manage the stress.

RECOGNIZE POTENTIAL PROBLEMS

It hasn't been that long since you last visited your parents, but now you're at their house and discover it's disheveled, or their mail is piling up or you see concerning cognitive changes. Now what? It's easy to feel overwhelmed and unsure of how to proceed. "People don't know what to do when it comes to the whole aging world, or how to wrap their heads around what to do next," says Deborah Feldman, M.S.W., L.C.S.W., who works to help with decisions for elderly clients and their families.

Arming yourself with facts and resources will keep you from spiraling into a worry cycle. Try your local library for research and reach out to local experts who can help you take action. "Local senior centers are a great first resource," Feldman advises. "They can direct you to which department of aging to contact. If they have a social worker on-site, they'll explain what services are available in your community."

GET KEY INFORMATION UP FRONT

Loverde suggests focusing on three important areas: money; housing; and getting legal paperwork in order. "If you do those three things, you're far ahead of the game," she says.

Too many people wait, only to find out the hard way their parents are running out of money. Once you discover what shape their finances are in, you'll be able to have a second conversation about what makes sense about their living arrangement. This might include staying where they are with additional help, moving closer to adult children, entering a retirement community or other options. Finally, get their legal paperwork in order. In some situations, families may

Everywhere you look there is someone tugging at your sleeve. I hear the stress.

—JOY LOVERDE, AUTHOR

hire an elder-care attorney to work on estate planning, health care decision-making and other important topics.

TALK THINGS OUT

You may think you're doing what's best, but there's a good chance you're stirring up resentment. "I believe what we have is not an elder-care problem today; it's a communication problem," says Loverde. "People go and visit their parents and tell them what to do. You cannot walk in the door and say, 'I'm in charge now.' They'll slam the door in your face."

Feldman agrees. "Everyone thinks about this time period as a role reversal, but it's not. You're a team working together." By approaching decisions and discussions with the right frame of mind, your parents may be more open to hearing you.

Before any big talk, ask yourself, "Am I the best person for this job? Or is there a sibling who has the ear of Mom and Dad, or an in-law, or an adult grandchild?" Whatever you want to discuss with your parents, Loverde warns against taking without giving. For example, if you feel your father should no longer be driving, don't just confiscate his car keys. Find out whether his community offers free or reduced-cost shuttles or taxis, or set him up with an account with a ride-sharing service like Uber or Lyft.

INVOLVE THE NEXT GENERATION

Interestingly, it's often our adult children who require more of our economic support. Pew Research Center reports that, for "adults in their 40s and 50s who have at least one child age 18 or older, fully 73 percent have provided at least some financial help in the past year to at least one such child." With increasing numbers of these so-called "boomerang" generation members living at home, being involved in our children's lives doesn't stop when they turn 18. "There is such a magic formula between grandchildren and grandparents," Loverde says. Can you look to them for help?

Younger kids can visit with you; a newly driving teen can gain practice behind the wheel by taking Granddad to the supermarket. And don't neglect adult children. Can they be the ones to talk to a grandparent who might not be listening to you? Think about how else you can involve them in a way that benefits all three generations.

CARE FOR YOURSELF, TOO

When you're needed by kids and parents, finding time for yourself is easier said than done. But it's important. "Make sure you have a friend that you can tell the truth to, or an online community where you can find other caregivers who can relate to your situation," says Loverde. Support groups are also helpful, so see if your local hospital offers groups for caregivers of patients with Alzheimer's or other conditions. "It's really good to be able to say it like it is," Loverde says. "There is something about talking to someone else who understands, is compassionate and isn't judging you."

No one is saying these relationships are easy, but with effort on all parts, these can be meaningful years together.

> Everyone thinks this is a time of role reversal, but you are a team working together.

—DEBORAH FELDMAN, M.S.W., L.C.S.W.

Use this time to deepen your relationships.

Holly Tarson and her husband moved closer to her husband's aging parents when their son was a toddler. "We had a number of years filled with holidays together and sweet memories. So we willingly entered the realm of the sandwich generation. In the past few years, the grandparents needed more care after a broken hip and Alzheimer's began to take their toll. It's sometimes a heavy load both in time and energy and in emotional wear and tear. But I know that full plate also represents all the people, young and old, in my life that I get to love. And I wouldn't want it any other way."

Aronson, the woman who stepped in after her father's sudden illness, agrees that her life is richer today. "After that initial crisis, our family pulled together in a way I never, ever thought possible. It's complicated, and it always will be, but there are so many gifts as well."

FIND SUPPORT

Caring for an aging parent while also managing your affairs at home isn't easy. These resources can help provide information when you need it most.

▶ **ELDERCARE LOCATOR**
(*eldercare.acl.gov*)
A great place to start, this site provides a wide variety of resources, from legal services and senior centers to home services, adult day programs, housing options, home-delivered meals, health insurance counseling, transportation access and more.

▶ **AREA AGENCY ON AGING** (*n4a.org*)
"This is a huge resource that you can access for help in the senior aging world," says Deborah Feldman, MSW, LCSW. The group acts as a clearinghouse for information and provides advice for navigating important discussions with your parents.

▶**FUTURE FILE** (*futurefile.com*)
This user-friendly website walks you through all of the documents you need to pull together for estate planning and finances, helping you organize important information in one easy-to-access place.

▶ **THE NATIONAL ACADEMY OF ELDER-LAW ATTORNEYS** (*naela.org*)
These specialty practitioners may be useful when it comes two planning for long-term care; deciphering Medicaid and Medicare coverage, insurance and more; health-care decision making; as well as drafting wills and estate planning.

▶ **CAREGIVER ACTION NETWORK**
(*caregiveraction.org*)
This active online community can give you comfort when you really need it. Find a wide variety of community chat threads, peer support and resources from the National Family Caregiver Association.

Make your visits a
multigenerational
opportunity.

Give your child
"struggle time" to
push through.

GENERATION STRESS

KIDS TODAY ARE MORE STRESSED THAN EVER—AND LESS EQUIPPED TO DEAL WITH IT. BUT YOU CAN HELP THEM LEARN TO ADAPT AND EVEN THRIVE WHEN THE GOING GETS TOUGH.

Making
mistakes
helps to build
resilience.

When I was 15, I'm pretty sure my biggest source of stress was whether my parents would finally allow me to get my own (land line) phone in my bedroom.

My twins are now 15, and I can't even begin to fathom the amount of pressure they face on a daily basis. Between worrying that their social media posts aren't worded exactly right (and then panicking about the number of "likes" they get); trying to keep on top of an ever-mounting pile of homework and fretting their grades aren't high enough; and squeezing countless practices, rehearsals, lessons and meetings into an already jam-packed schedule, it's a wonder they are able to function at all.

As a parent, I naturally worry about my kids' mental health as much as their physical well-being. And I know I'm not alone in my concern that my kids are coping with more stress than ever. "The level of stress today does seem to be much higher than among previous generations," notes Kate Lund, Ph.D., a clinical psychologist based in Seattle, and author of *Bounce: Help Your Child Build Resilience and Thrive in School, Sports and Life*. "There's a lot more emphasis on having to be the best at something as opposed to just enjoying the process."

And the stress can start early. Even very young kids start to feel stress at higher levels, adds Lund, especially if they are more conscious of their own feelings, also known as having emotional intelligence. Stress seems to really ratchet up in the tween and teens years, however, and while it's more prominent among girls, boys have their issues to face as well.

"Kids are becoming increasingly more sensitive to different kinds of traumas today," notes Ari Yares, Ph.D., a licensed psychologist based in Potomac, Maryland. "They are facing a lot of things today that we didn't have to worry about 30 years ago." That's especially true of social pressures, where every post and comment is carefully analyzed, and issues like cyberbullying have become all too common.

FEAR OF FAILURE

Parents may also unintentionally be making it more difficult for kids to navigate stress. "Kids have always had to face different forms of stress, but the difference today is that by overprotecting our kids they've become less adept at coping with challenges," says James Millhouse, Ph.D., a licensed psychologist based in Atlanta and the author of *The Parents Manual of Sports Psychology*. "That 'everyone gets a trophy' mentality that we often apply to kids' activities means that they don't necessarily understand that it's OK to fail."

Developing effective coping mechanisms may, in fact, be one of the best lessons we can teach our kids. "We want our kids to be motivated to push through difficult situations and apply themselves as effectively as possible. Sometimes a little stress can be a good way to do that," adds Millhouse. And since we all have to face stress at some point in our lives, the better equipped they are to handle that pressure, the more easily kids will be able to thrive in even difficult situations.

But as a parent, how do you know when that pressure is too much? The signs aren't always obvious, but there are a few characteristics that might appear. "Your

A little stress can help your child learn to push through difficult situations.

— JAMES MILLHOUSE, PH.D.

child might always seem to be worried, or not able to see the joy in what's around her. If it seems that it's hard to pull anything positive out of them, it's likely that they've reached a tipping point," says Lund.

It's almost never too early to give your child the tools he or she needs to increase resilience, build confidence and conquer stress. "You don't have to expose them to pressure, but giving even small challenges can help, whether that's completing a puzzle without help or navigating a playdate without being overly supervised," says Millhouse. Here are some more ways you can help your child feel strong in even high-stress situations.

▶ Don't shy away from the hard stuff.

One surefire way to feel confident under pressure is to embrace challenges when they come. "Kids need to learn that not succeeding the first time around isn't the end of the world," says Lund. "Challenges are nothing more than opportunities for growth. When you try and try again, you'll develop a more flexible way of thinking." After a while, she adds, kids will internalize that they have an ability to succeed and call upon that resolve when times get tough.

▶ Sign up for (some) activities.

Whether it's soccer, chess club or the school play, encourage your kids to get involved with an organized activity. Millhouse is a big fan of youth sports, which he says is a place to practice all the skills you'll use later in life (like learning how to win and lose, and teamwork), but you don't need to be nurturing a future Olympian to see the benefits. "When kids are exposed to a wide range of activities,

they can find where they may excel and develop a passion—and that can ultimately give them more confidence," agrees Lund.

▶ Think positive.

Whether you're taking an exam, dealing with a bully or facing a pitch at the plate, your attitude makes a big difference in how you respond. "You want to get into what we call an ideal performance state," says Millhouse. With it, you feel confident, relaxed but alert, and feeling like you are going to be successful. "We teach this to athletes but it applies to any stressful situation," he explains. To start, focus on the process, not the outcome. That means concentrating on what you are doing (like taking a test) and not the outcome (whether you will pass or fail). Positive self-talk is also important. "Instead of thinking, 'This test is so hard,' think about, 'It will be a challenge but I know I am up to the task.' You want to believe that things will go well," he adds.

▶ Learn how to be mindful.

As adults, we've started to embrace the practice of mindfulness, or learning how to be more fully present. Very young kids are naturally mindful (ever see how fixated a toddler can get watching a squirrel?) but we tend to lose that heightened awareness as we get older. "Mindful practices can be highly effective among tweens and teens," says Yares. He likes to teach kids to engage in the "STOP" technique, especially when they start to feel stressed. "Stop what you are doing and slow down. Take a few breaths, inhaling for four counts, holding your breath for four counts, then exhaling for four counts; repeat that four times. Observe what's going on and how you are feeling. And finally, proceed and

> "Mindful practices can be highly effective stress reducers for teens and tweens."
>
> —ARI YARES PH.D.

try to think about the most important thing you should pay attention to right now." This technique helps to push the pause button and pull you into the present moment, he adds.

Lund works with her young clients on a similar form of mindfulness training called Heart Math. Although the program is tied to a video game, it incorporates deep breathing while also focusing on something that actively makes you happy. "Once you learn to do it, you can call up that sensation whenever you are starting to feel stressed. It's a mind-body technique that helps to actively manage emotions," she says.

▶ Have an open conversation.
"It's important to talk with your kids about stress in general," says Lund. Keeping the lines of communication open about if and when your child is encountering high levels of stress means your child will be more likely to come to you when she hits a rocky patch. While you're at it, share your own experience when it comes to coping with an uncomfortable situation, whether that was an argument you had at work or a mistake you made during the day and how you fixed it. "This way your child doesn't feel like everything hard that happens is the end of the world," adds Lund.

▶ Model good behavior.
How do you react to stress? If you handle it in a positive way, chances are your kids will also be more adept at coping. "We often take our own stress out on our kids—yelling at them to clean up after a tough day, or being curt," says Yares. "It's important to get your own stress under control in order to help your child."

3 COPING STRATEGIES FOR KIDS

What your kids consider stressful is probably a lot different from what makes you anxious. Here's how to help them face a few common sources of stress.

▶ **ACADEMIC PRESSURE** Plenty of kids get stressed out about academics, even when they're in elementary school. "The rule of thumb should be no more than 10 minutes of homework per grade level," says licensed psychologist Ari Yares. Keep an eye on how much time your children are spending doing schoolwork and whether it's productive time or if they are just spinning their wheels. "If you really think they're not getting anywhere, tell them they've worked on it long enough—it's OK to reach out to a teacher and communicate that your child may be having difficulties."

▶ **SOCIAL STRESS** "This is where those open lines of communication are so important," notes Yares. Be aware of who your child's friends are, where they are going and what they are doing. "Ask the questions or you'll never get the answers," he adds. You can also talk about how you handle awkward or difficult social situations, such as dealing with an annoying coworker or resolving a conflict. "That opens the door for kids to share their own thoughts."

▶ **JAM-PACKED SCHEDULE** No doubt, kids today are highly overscheduled. So do what you can to carve in some family downtime. Make a weekly family game or movie night; plan a weekend walk; have a dinner that everyone must sit down to. "Make that sacred time and stick to it so you can be sure your family is spending time together and not always jetting all over the place," says Yares.

WARNING SIGNS OF STRESS

Worried your child's stress levels are affecting his health? Look for the following red flags that signal more action may be required on your part:

▶ Drop in grades

▶ Change in diet

▶ Difficulty sleeping

▶ Frequent headaches or stomachaches

▶ Unexplained fears of isolation

▶ Loss of interest in activities he or she once loved

▶ Experimentation with drugs and alcohol

A TEENAGER'S GUIDE TO STRESS

It's time. Time to step on the ice, for the puck to drop. I'm a goalie on an all-girls hockey team, and the games can be intense. But even as the action starts to take shape, deadlines, worries and unfinished conversations begin to push into my thoughts. Formulas for quadratic equations, remembering to text a friend and thinking about how little sleep I had last night bubble up in my brain. Then I realize that I need to pay close attention to what's happening on the ice and whether the puck is going to come my way. So I push these distractions away and focus on what is happening right in front of me. I do my best to take things one step—one play, one moment—at a time.

I'm pretty busy on most days, so managing stress can be a challenge. Sometimes, it feels that there just aren't enough hours in the day to get everything done. One night, I might get home from hockey and realize I forgot to practice a song for my orchestra concert the next day. Or I'll spend hours procrastinating on the internet before realizing I forgot to text a study guide to my friend.

I'm 15, and most of these are just typical teenage high school experiences. We're all trying to balance social lives and academics, learning to handle the responsibilities that come with getting older. I've seen how my friends and classmates handle stress. Some blow everything off until the last minute; others meticulously plan out what they are doing. And some focus so much on doing everything perfectly that they eventually crack under pressure.

While, of course, there are things that may not be under our control, a lot of what we do is relative to how we approach things. If I don't plan out what I have to do, or I have unrealistically high expectations like needing to get a perfect score on a test or keeping the opponent from scoring in a game, I may end up in tears.

Instead, I try to stay positive whenever I can and steer clear of negative thoughts. That's not to say I never get stressed: I love feeling just a little nervous before I step onto the ice because that means I am dialed in and ready to put my best effort forward. But when I sit down to take a test, or pick up my flute to play at a recital, I know that I've done my best to prepare and while I may make a mistake, it will be OK. It's all about finding the balance between using stress as a motivator and not allowing it to get overwhelming. Ultimately, I know that no matter what I do, there will always be another chance to make it better.

—*Layla Shaffer, age 15, New York City*

Kids face stress from a wide variety of sources.

Take time to digest the news before reacting.

HEALTH

COPING WITH A CRISIS

WHETHER YOU OR A LOVED ONE HAS RECEIVED SOME
SCARY NEWS FROM YOUR DOCTOR, USE THESE
SEVEN STRATEGIES TO ALLEVIATE SOME OF THE STRESS.

There's no getting around it: A health crisis is stressful. Whether a test has come back with questionable results, you've received a scary health diagnosis or are in the middle of treatment, or you have a loved one who's experiencing any of the above, coping with a health crisis can ratchet anxiety up to epic levels. After all, a health crisis cannot be ignored, brushed aside or "deep-breathed" away (although deep breaths can always help!). In addition, physical symptoms or medical treatments can also affect your mood, making it tough to parse out exactly how you're feeling. And a health crisis can make you feel powerless, which can cause your mind to begin to spin to "what if" scenarios.

But in the middle of so many unknowns, experts say it is entirely possible to find some inner peace. Here, you'll find seven techniques that can help you lower stress levels and cope more effectively with the health crisis you or someone you love may be facing.

TAKE YOUR TIME

This is where those deep breaths come in. If you or a loved one has just gotten a diagnosis from the doctor, you may feel you have to move right away. And while you can't push aside treatment for weeks or months down the road, you generally have time to get a second opinion or take a moment to sit with the news before you spring into action, says Pamela Ginsberg, Ph.D., a staff psychologist for the Doylestown Health System in Doylestown, Pennsylvania.

"We're always told never to make a decision when we're stressed. And of course, when you get a diagnosis like cancer or another life-threatening illness, you're likely at your most stressed, and then tasked with making treatment decisions," says Ginsberg. "But even a few hours can make a big difference in giving you the mental space you need to effectively make decisions regarding your treatment plan." If you feel like a talk with your doctor is becoming incomprehensible as your mind spins, let them know you feel overwhelmed and ask them for a few minutes. "Controlling the timeline a bit can help you feel more in control," says Ginsberg.

LOOK TO THE PAST

While you may have never dealt with a health crisis, you've likely dealt with other types of stressful situations in your past. Ginsberg says how you handled those experiences may give you a template for how you'll instinctually respond to this one. Did you isolate yourself, when retrospectively, you wished you'd reached out more? Did you find yourself going into overdrive researching whatever situation you were facing, and how did that make you feel? Not only can the "I've gone through hard times before, and I can handle this one now" perspective make you feel more in control, it may also help you feel less disoriented about your situation, says Ginsberg. Bibliotherapy—reading books about others who have faced a similar situation—may also be helpful. For example, *When Breath Becomes Air* by Paul Kalanithi and *The Bright Hour* by Nina Riggs are two recent best-selling autobiographies by writers who faced

Give yourself some mental space to effectively make decisions.

—PAMELA GINSBERG, PH.D.

terminal cancer diagnoses and which are often read in hospital support groups.

WIDEN YOUR RESOURCES

More and more hospitals offer mental health support for patients, spouses and family members going through critical illness or injury. If your doctor doesn't offer up resources, ask about them yourself. "Many oncology units have a social worker on staff, and the same goes for many other serious illnesses," says Ginsberg. If you or a loved one is in the hospital, ask about meeting with a social worker, who can help point you in the direction of resources that can help you cope with stress and break down any mental roadblocks that might come up. Hospitals may also host support groups, which can be invaluable, says Gregory Garber, M.S.W., director of oncology support services at the Kimmel Cancer Center at Thomas Jefferson University. "There's a lot to be said about being with people who have coped with the same crisis you're facing." There's no obligation to go more than once, but it's worth trying out.

Loved ones can provide much needed support.

Organizing your
to-dos can give you
a sense of control.

CREATE A TO-DO LIST (THEN FARM IT OUT)

Whatever you're coping with, chances are as soon as friends and family hear the news, you'll be getting texts asking you to reach out for help. Take people up on the offer. One way to break the stress cycle is to focus on something you can control, says Garber. Write a list of all the "ordinary" things that need to be done in your house: getting the dog walked, the kids picked up from school, meals on the table, the car's oil changed—whatever occurs to you. The next time people ask how they can help, refer to that list. It can also be beneficial to appoint a helper "point person" who can parse through requests and assign out tasks. This can be a family member or friend who may not actively be involved in dealing with the health crisis, but knows enough about you, your family, and household that you can trust him or her to be your de-facto "household manager" while you're focused on other things. This way, not only are you getting things done, you're also clearing your own plate to have the mental space to focus on whatever challenges lie ahead. You can also set this up digitally: While some medical-specific apps exist, you can always use a Google calendar or a free digital organization tool like Trello to create lists, assign tasks and invite friends and family, so they can assign themselves tasks and communicate when the task will be done.

CONTROL THE FLOW OF INFO

Repeat after us: Dr. Google is not your doctor. "It's easy to go down the rabbit hole of what-if scenarios when researching a diagnosis on the internet, but it's important to remember that your doctor should always be your primary point of contact," says Garber. If you do want to research, remember that credible advice is generally found on websites from a university (.edu) or a research organization specific to the health crisis you're currently grappling with. If you do Google, check in with how you're feeling, and close your laptop if you realize you're feeling anxious. If you're sharing info about the health crisis with your friends and family, a closed, invite-only Facebook group or a website like Caringbridge can be a helpful place to post updates and general info on how you or your loved one is doing, so you don't have to respond to dozens of texts a day.

FIND ANOTHER FOCUS

It's easy for a health crisis to become all-consuming. If you can, find something positive in the future to focus on that has nothing to do with the illness. Maybe it's purchasing tickets for an upcoming show in your town, or planning a post-hospital discharge vacation. Or maybe it's fulfilling a personal challenge, like finally reading *Anna Karenina*, learning Spanish via the Duolingo app or taking up crochet. These sorts of activities can become your go-to in the waiting room, during treatments or when you are at the hospital, giving you something positive to focus on that reminds you your life is so much larger than just the health diagnosis. If your loved one is facing a diagnosis, consider gifting them activity gifts—a journal and beautiful pens, two copies of a book so both of you can read and form a de facto book club during long treatments, a "learn to knit" kit—rather than flowers or food.

It's natural for your mind to go to dark places.

—GREGORY GARBER, M.S.W.

Don't be afraid to ask questions of your health-care helpers.

LET YOUR MIND GO TO THE WORST (FOR A BIT)

Of course, everyone around you is going to tell you to think positively. And if your loved ones are facing an illness, you also may be tempted to tell them to look on the bright side, keep their chin up and know they'll get better. But that can be counterproductive, says Garber. "It's natural for your mind to go to dark places, and it's so much better to allow yourself to explore those thoughts, and find a safe space to talk about them, than brush them aside or try to ignore them." If you've been diagnosed with a life-threatening illness, it's OK to imagine what might happen if you were to die. "Remember, imagining it won't make it come true," says Garber. Allowing yourself the freedom to explore these thoughts makes them less forbidden, which takes away their power, and allows you to focus on the here and now. If a spouse, family member or friend is going through a health crisis, let them talk about what might happen if they were to die. It's not a sign that they're giving up; it's a sign of trust and a conversation that can help make them feel less panicked by whatever the future may hold.

CRISIS RESOURCES

▶ **NATIONAL NONPROFITS FOR THE ILLNESS** Many illnesses have nonprofits dedicated to research, funding and patient advocacy, as well as resources for patients and caregivers. This can be a great first stop for medically accurate information, links to area support groups and smaller nonprofits that may be local or have a more specific focus. For example, the American Cancer Society (*cancer.org*) and American Heart Association (*heart.org*) can be good resources—your doctor may also have suggestions.

▶ **CARINGBRIDGE** Rather than constantly sending the same text or email updates to your friends and family, disseminate all the information in one place. Use the site to create a journal updating others about your condition or that of your loved one or use it to list things you may need. (*caringbridge.org*)

▶ **MEAL TRAIN** In times of crisis, people often think of offering food for comfort. This service allows you, a friend or family member to put together a list of volunteer meals so your family always has a hot meal to eat and you have one less thing to worry about. After all, no one wants five casseroles in their fridge at once. (*mealtrain.com*)

▶ **LOTSA HELPING HANDS** The popular planning site and app is easy to use and allows caregivers to coordinate schedules, lists and communication in the midst of a health crisis. (*lotsahelpinghands.com*)

▶ **CARE CALENDAR** Another tool that can be helpful to coordinate any errands, to-do lists or needs, this one includes the option to create a registry of tangible needs, like gift cards and groceries. It can be helpful for some families to have two calendars—one for their inner circle that includes more personal to-dos like babysitting and rides to appointments, and one that can be shared with a church or school community that may include more generalized things like a meal delivery service. (*carecalendar.com*)

Concerns from climate change to politics can create an undercurrent of stress.

WORLDWIDE WORRIES

SOCIETAL STRESSORS LIKE POLITICS, CLIMATE CHANGE AND TERRORISM ARE TAKING A GREATER TOLL ON OUR PSYCHE THAN EVER BEFORE, BUT THERE ARE STEPS YOU CAN TAKE TO EASE YOUR CONCERNS AND GAIN CONTROL.

Scroll through Facebook and there's a pretty good chance you'll see an in-your-face political rant from your uncle who voted for the candidate you opposed. Turn on the TV and there's news about a terrorist attack. Pick up a paper and there's a story about the latest school shooting. It's not your imagination—it really is getting harder to escape the constant negative news cycle.

Thanks to our multiplatform lives, we're experiencing 24/7 news coverage in ways we never have before—and not all of it is good. "Social media platforms, which began as ways to connect with friends and share family photos, are now one of the main ways that people 'get the news,'" says Farrah Hauke, Psy.D., a licensed psychologist in Scottsdale, Arizona. "While more information is always a good thing, some of the information that is reported is inaccurate or biased."

It can also be incendiary—and created to rile up emotions. With a computer screen of anonymity in front of us, many people feel emboldened to share their views in ways they never would in person, such as attacking and name-calling when others do not share their views, adds Hauke. Plus, all of this animosity appears to be good for ratings. "The media is keenly aware that reporting stories that get us worked up and focus on negativity are much more likely to attract viewers—and thus sell commercials. As a result, we are seeing media sources across the political spectrum produce more divisive and commentary-based content as opposed to neutral and fact-based reporting," says Hauke.

All of this exposure can ultimately wear us down. "People have always had political concerns, and a lot of these societal issues have been around and unaddressed for long periods of time—but as our level of awareness has increased, the amount of time we spend thinking and engaging with it has as well," says Kelsey Torgerson, L.C.S.W., a St. Louis-based therapist who specializes in adolescent anxiety. "We get burned out when we spend too much time or energy without taking care of ourselves, and then we're a lot less useful than before. This is something that everyone needs to take into consideration: the line between engaging too much versus engaging the right amount."

In addition to simply shutting off the TV, stepping away from the computer and turning off your phone when the news gets to be too much, take a deep breath and try these coping strategies for some of the biggest issues that affect us today.

THE CONCERN
The economy

With the ups and downs of the market, you can sometimes watch your retirement fund shrinking right before your eyes, and the same goes for property values. While the global market has been in flux, you can get a grip on your finances by doing some digging. Focus on your personal financial health and build up your financial literacy. Torgerson recommends budgeting apps like You Need A Budget or Mint to track how you're spending your money and why. And remember, the economy is likely just a short-term problem, so weather the storm for now and know that it will bounce back soon enough.

59%

Percentage of adults in the U.S. who say the current social divisiveness causes them stress

Don't agree with the opinion of others? Learning to build tolerance can help.

THE CONCERN
Political discourse

It's not uncommon for a family dinner to turn into a hot debate when the subject of politics comes up. Keep things civil by knowing in advance what you are and are not comfortable discussing and in what setting or context. "This will allow you to set boundaries and limits in advance with friends and family," Hauke says. For example, perhaps your nephew's second birthday party is not the time or place you wish to discuss politics; if that is the case, you can tell others in advance, or, when these conversations arise, let them know of your boundary. "Say, 'I know you are very passionate about topic X, but I would like to spend my time focused on little Timmy right now; maybe we can discuss this later?' If others cannot, or do not, respect the boundary you have set, take a break from the situation by removing yourself from the conversation or politely excusing yourself," she adds.

In times of crisis, stay in touch with your community.

THE CONCERN
Climate change

Listening to the state of the planet and thinking about where things may be heading next can feel terrifying, but taking action can help. Do your research on what impacts the environment and spread awareness among friends and family. You can make a difference. "On the micro level, try walking to work, using public transportation, recycling and researching other small changes you can make as an individual," Torgerson says. "On a mezzo level, see if your school or workplace is open to instituting changes to recycling or incentivizing environmentally friendly policies. On a macro level, participate in town hall meetings and stick with it. Oftentimes, politicians won't change what's happening unless they know that you and others like you are really vocal about what needs to be changed."

THE CONCERN
Terrorism

Lately it feels like there is one attack after another. "It's scary, but when it comes to threats of terrorism, radical acceptance can really be huge," Torgerson says. "Realistically, in a terrorist attack, there's little we can do. We can't predict it. We know it's relatively unlikely for us to encounter an active shooter—but it might happen. Try just sitting with that thought, without letting it emotionally impact you. It might happen, it might happen, it might happen.... Usually, the more we sit with this thought, the less emotional impact it has. It's like getting your fingers stuck in a finger trap. If you try to jerk and pull away from the thought, it tightens its grip on you. Only by moving your two fingers together, by noticing and accepting the thought, can you free yourself from the trap." To give yourself some more feeling of security, encourage your workplace to take necessary security precautions, and volunteer to help out with relief efforts when possible.

The constant drumbeat of violence can feel overwhelming.

THE CONCERN
Social media

From angry tweets to political rants on Facebook that don't match your values, social media can be a virtual land mine when it comes to inducing emotional stress. So start to curate your feeds. "Ask yourself why you joined social media in the first place, and then edit and streamline your friends, contacts, likes and followed pages and people to match this," Hauke says. "One might also consider unfriending or unfollowing those individuals in our online lives who do not bring us happiness or respect." If certain types of posts are too much for you to handle, you can also click "Do not show these type of posts" on your Instagram and Facebook feeds. And don't be afraid to shut your phone off for a few hours (or even a few days). Research shows that taking a digital detox can go a long way in helping to improve self-esteem and reduce both anxiety and depression, adds Hauke.

Getting involved in a cause you believe in offers a sense of control.

MOST COMMON CAUSES OF STRESS REGARDING THE NATION

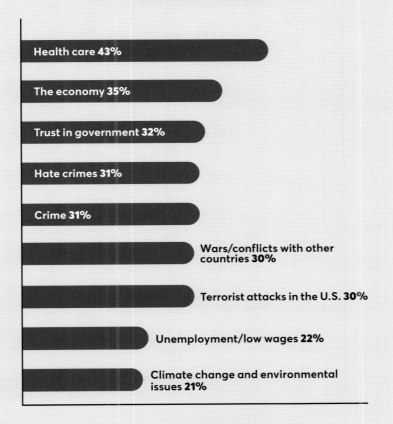

Health care 43%

The economy 35%

Trust in government 32%

Hate crimes 31%

Crime 31%

Wars/conflicts with other countries 30%

Terrorist attacks in the U.S. 30%

Unemployment/low wages 22%

Climate change and environmental issues 21%

Source: American Psychological Association

PART THREE

LEARNING HOW TO COPE

YOU CAN'T ELIMINATE ALL THE STRESS
FROM YOUR LIFE, BUT YOU CAN
MANAGE MOST SITUATIONS
BY EMPLOYING A FEW KEY STRATEGIES.

Go for it! Over time, what used to seem scary won't be anymore.

THE SECRET OF STRESS INOCULATION

LEARNING HOW TO IDENTIFY THE SIGNS OF STRESS AND THEN DELIBERATELY EXPOSING YOURSELF TO IT CAN HELP YOU GET A HANDLE ON ANXIETY BEFORE IT GETS OUT OF CONTROL.

Stress inoculation is about learning to regulate your response so you can be effective.

—URSZULA KLICH, PH.D.

Think back to a time when you were about to do something entirely new and at least a little scary. Maybe it was your first day of high school, or moving into the college dorm. Perhaps it was your first real attempt at navigating the dating world, or having to speak in front of a group of people. Or maybe you had to take an overseas flight, or deal with a high-stress project at work.

No matter what the experience, there's a good chance you had more than your fair share of butterflies in your stomach. Your mind may have raced with thoughts of self-doubt or dread—Will I let everyone down? What if something goes wrong? Do they like me? Am I doing all right? Did I make the right decision? When will this be over?

For most of us, once we started the experience and got used to whatever we were doing, our stress levels began to drop. Whether it took a few hours or a few months, we gradually started to build our confidence and felt more secure in our abilities, whether that's becoming more comfortable at public speaking or settling into a routine at a new job or school.

This process is a snapshot of what psychologists often refer to as "stress inoculation"—the idea that over time, as we increase our ability to regulate our responses to a given stressor, we're better able to handle and persevere through it.

Think of it like getting immunized against stress. You expose yourself gradually to a stressor, just as you're exposed to little bits of a virus when you get an immunization shot. The idea is that your stress-management system (all those coping skills and other self-regulation resources you know how to tap) is prompted to kick into gear. Gradually, by such graded exposure (you don't want to throw yourself into a very stressful situation all at once) you develop a greater tolerance for that stressor.

Often, this comes as a natural result of learning new skills that make what may have once seemed insurmountable start to feel more manageable. Sometimes you can do this on your own. And sometimes you need some extra help (think: from a therapist) to develop these skills (no shame in that!).

Conceived in the 1970s by psychologist Donald H. Meichenbaum, Ph.D., stress inoculation is informed by cognitive psychology, which focuses on how we think, problem-solve and perceive ourselves and the world around us. It involves three basic steps, explains Sal Raichbach, Psy.D., L.C.S.W., a therapist at Ambrosia Treatment Center in Port St. Lucie, Florida, who regularly counsels clients through the process. Read along for some guidance on how to bolster your own psychological immune system —on or off a therapist's couch.

STEP 1
Learn the signs of stress.
"The first step of stress inoculation involves learning about the general nature of stress, starting to understand and recognize its symptoms and being able to differentiate between a stressful situation and the response we're having to it," explains Raichbach. This lets you step back, realize you are dealing with stress and observe how your body and mind are reacting.

Most stressful reactions have both

physical and psychological components. Physical reactions may include restlessness, an increase in heart rate, sweaty or clammy palms, clenching your jaw, hunching your shoulders, the sensation of having butterflies in your stomach, feeling nauseous or losing your appetite, or feeling extreme weakness or fatigue. Psychological reactions include thoughts, beliefs and behaviors that crop up in response to being stressed—and often serve to exacerbate it. Think: self-defeating statements and self-criticism: "I should be better at this by now," "I'll never get all of this done," or "I'm such a disappointment."

Even if this seems pretty basic, recognizing and coming to understand the symptoms of stress is a huge and important step toward getting it under control. Be sure you've gotten sufficient practice at knowing your personal stress signs and symptoms before progressing to the next step, says Raichbach. The better you're acquainted with them, the better able you'll be to manage them.

STEP 2
Practice your coping skills.
Once you've started to recognize how you react under stress, the next step is to practice ways to handle these responses. Ideally, this is in conditions that are relatively relaxed, whether that's with a therapist, in a support group or on your own, says Raichbach. Learned and rehearsed skills will vary based on your own needs, he says, but can include everything from emotion-regulation skills (like diaphragmatic breathing, mindfulness and relaxation techniques) to simple time-management and basic budgeting skills, assertiveness training (think: learning how to say "no" when you need to and setting limits with others), physical self-care (eating well and exercising a bit more have been shown to help combat anxiety and stress) and sleep hygiene (getting enough of it, for starters, which has also been found to help reduce anxiety and stress).

One very important skill is the ability to reinterpret those physiological symptoms of stress not as signs of an emotional apocalypse but as signals that your body is gearing up to best prepare you for an energy-requiring task, says Urszula Klich, Ph.D., a clinical psychologist based in Atlanta who leads wellness workshops nationwide. For example: Instead of "Oh my God, my heart's racing and I'll never be able to get it under control," step back and think, "Oh, isn't that interesting—my heart rate is increasing. My body must be mobilizing its resources to make sure I perform at my peak."

"The idea is to shift your perception and adjust your attitude toward the stress you're experiencing," she says. This enables you to be less reactive to the stress you're experiencing, which only serves to make it worse, and more responsive to it, "by drawing in some relaxation and mindfulness techniques to moderate that level of stress so it doesn't get the better of you," Klich explains.

STEP 3
Get out there.
Once you're able to sufficiently call forth all of the skills that you've practiced in a relatively safe space, you can then introduce yourself to situations that bring you closer to your actual source of stress. Start small and build up gradually, Klich advises. For someone who is afraid

of flying, this may mean driving to an airport and practicing slow, diaphragmatic breathing in the car. Have a fear of public speaking but a presentation coming up at work? Ask a few friends or your family to listen while you practice aloud in your living room or other environment that feels safe and comfortable.

A common misconception when it comes to stress inoculation, Klich warns, is that it will be beneficial to just throw yourself into uncomfortable situations with the hope that you'll eventually get over the anxiety regarding them. This may work for some people, she says, but you have to be very careful—especially if you're prone to more anxiety—to not overload yourself during the entire stress-inoculation practice.

Like an athlete who has trained for an upcoming race or important game, you can call upon the practice you've already done to help you navigate a stressful situation. Trust yourself to know what you can handle, and give yourself a break if you need to take it a little more slowly, Klich says. "The more patient and accepting you are of yourself, the more likely you are to succeed in being able to call forth those self-regulation skills that will enable you to handle whatever stressors you hope to be able to navigate." Stress inoculation isn't about the avoidance of stress altogether, Klich adds. "It's about learning to regulate your physiological and mental response to it so that you can be more effective and successful in stressful situations."

25%

Percentage of people who say they have a fear of public speaking— but with a little practice you can conquer it!

A few deep breaths can kick off the relaxation response.

BREATHE DEEP

In need of a quick, drug-free release of anxiety? One of the easiest ways to reduce stress—and one we often forget is always on hand—is to breathe. It may sound overly simplistic, but science backs its efficacy in dialing down how keyed-up and overwhelmed we feel.

Deep breathing—and let's be clear here: this means diaphragmatic (or "belly") breathing, not chest breathing—cues our nervous system to shift away from fight-or-flight mode and into rest-and-digest mode, explains Urszula Klich, Ph.D. (Chest breathing, by contrast, can trigger hyperventilation and, as a result, can increase stress and anxiety by triggering an increase in the stress hormones coursing through our bloodstream.) The next time you're freaking out, pause (excuse yourself from a situation if you have to) and take 10 "slow and low" deep breaths. Note how different you feel. No, breathing can't solve all of your problems. But it can physiologically enable you to handle them more calmly and clearheadedly.

Practicing staying in the moment keeps stress at bay.

THE POWER OF THE MIND

MINDFUL PRACTICES CAN HELP REDUCE
STRESS AND ENHANCE WELL-BEING—AND IT
DOESN'T TAKE A LOT TO SEE RESULTS.

We all know what it feels like to be stressed. Your stomach feels like it's in knots. Maybe your palms start to sweat or your face turns red. Perhaps you start to breathe more rapidly, or your heart rate speeds up. And your mind is racing about what you need to do next. Stress, in short, can be highly physical as well as emotional.

Then think about what it feels like when you stop and take a deep breath. You fill your lungs with air, and simply concentrate on the act of inhaling and exhaling as slowly and deeply as possible. More often than not, that stress soon starts to melt away, and you begin to feel more calm and in control.

You've just practiced one of the fundamental tenets of mindfulness— the act of staying in the moment rather than reacting to a potential threat. This activates the body's parasympathetic nervous system, which helps to halt the production of stress hormones and increases the relaxation response.

WHAT IS MINDFULNESS?

Mindfulness is generally defined as nonjudgmental awareness of the present moment. It's about stopping the whirlwind of thoughts that fill your mind and taking a moment to consciously quiet down. "Mindfulness is a way to get us out of our reactive mind and those patterns that can keep you racing from one thought to the next," says David Dillard-Wright, Ph.D., an associate professor at the University of South Carolina Aiken and author of *The Boundless Life Challenge: 90 Days to Transform Your Mindset—and Your*

Learn how to get control over your anxiety and live happier.

You can practice mindfulness anywhere you go.

Life. "It allows you to step back and take a moment to think about what you are doing and why."

We've practiced mindfulness for thousands of years, in one form or another, but it's only in more modern times that we've come to appreciate what it can offer in the way of relieving stress and anxiety. When you are in the midst of a stressful situation—or when you're dealing with chronic stress day after day—mindfulness can give you the tools to step aside and gain perspective on the situation.

You not only feel calmer, experts say, but your body starts to undergo real physical changes that will last. "Our brains evolved to have a quick reaction to stress. That's

the fight-or-flight symptom that we all know," explains psychotherapist Linda Miles, whose most recent book, *Change Your Story, Change Your Brain*, explores the power of mindfulness. But when we face so many perceived threats on a daily basis (long commutes, jam-packed schedules, never-ending responsibilities), it's difficult to turn that switch off. "With mindfulness, you can stop, notice what you are thinking, and start to shut down those fear centers that are on overdrive," she notes. "Instead of just reacting to either fight or flee, we can say, 'Wait a minute—am I really in danger here?' We can learn to make better decisions and see possibilities instead of acting on our immediate gut reaction."

Activities that specifically focus on exercising kindness and appreciation actually prompt the brain to produce the feel-good chemicals oxytocin and dopamine, while at the same time decreasing the secretion of the stress hormones cortisol and adrenaline, adds Miles. Those chemicals may be important for short-term stressful situations (like running away from an attacker) but over the long term they can lead to numerous health concerns, from heart disease and high blood pressure to GI issues.

FINDING A PATH

Mindfulness can be a big word that conveys many meanings, and it can be confusing to figure out just what exactly we mean when we say we need to be more mindful. "But it doesn't have to be so daunting," says Dillard-Wright. "You just need to find little breaks during the day, like when you're at lunch or trying to settle in at night, and find a few moments to try and quiet the mind."

There's no one single way to be mindful—in fact, the beauty of mindfulness is that each of us can have our own approach. The following exercises may be a good way to get started.

▶ Create a space in your home.

You don't need to turn your spare room into a meditation studio, but having some space set aside where you know you can sit and be calm can be enormously helpful, says Dillard-Wright. "All you really need is a chair or a cushion and some peace and quiet," he notes. It can be in your bedroom, living room, study or just a little window nook. Some people may want to decorate it with objects that remind them to be mindful, whether that's a statue of an angel or Buddha, a vase of fresh flowers, a picture of the ocean or an aromatic diffuser.

▶ Take a deep breath.

One of the best ways to engage in mindfulness is to simply start with some deep-breathing exercises. "It really just involves slowing down your breath and inhaling and exhaling deeper than normal," says Dillard-Wright. "We use our breath as a way of getting in touch with our bodies." Keep your eyes open or closed (many say it's easier to focus with your eyes closed). There are many ways to incorporate deep-breathing exercises but a good one to start is to simply take an exaggerated breath. Inhale deeply through your nose for three counts. Then hold your breath for two counts, and exhale through your mouth for four counts. Focus on your breathing itself, such as how your chest rises and falls or the way the air feels coming through your nostrils. If your mind starts to wander, that's OK—just notice that it's happening and then gently bring your attention back to focus on your breath.

▶ Be positive.

Sit somewhere quiet, close your eyes, and recall a time when you felt loved and cherished. Remember how serene and blissful you felt, says Miles. Now imagine that positive energy bathing your body. "Positive emotions like this can release some of those feel-good chemicals that will help relax you further and buffer you against stress," she notes.

Even taking little breaks during the day can help quiet the mind.

—DAVID DILLARD-WRIGHT, PH.D.

▶ **Express gratitude.**

Focusing on what you're grateful for can help draw you away from a stressful situation and make you feel calmer. "When you deliberately focus on the blessings of the present moment and notice what's good, your whole outlook shifts to be more positive," says Dillard-Wright. Need help getting started? He recommends making a list (mental or physical) of five to 10 things you feel grateful for. "It can be as simple as being grateful for that cup of coffee you had this morning, or as big as feeling like your work today was fulfilling."

▶ **Find a phrase.**

Mantras have been used for thousands of years as a way to help reduce stress and enhance a sense of mindfulness. "A mantra can be a word, a syllable, a phrase or a sound that is repeated several times as a way to help you connect and feel the energy within and around you," explains Sherianna Boyle, author of *Mantras Made Easy: Mantras for Happiness, Peace, Prosperity, and More* and a yoga and meditation teacher based in Barnstable, Massachusetts. "Choose whatever phrase, word or sound that you are drawn to," says Boyle. You may want to pick something that's relatively short and easy to remember. Miles recommends a two-word phrase, such as "Big" (said or thought as you inhale) and "Calm" (said or thought as you exhale).

▶ **Do a body scan.**

Actively focusing on different areas of your body, from your feet to your face, helps increase awareness of your body and can reduce stress and tension. Try this brief exercise from the Greater Good Science Center at the University of California, Berkeley:

Get into a comfortable, seated position (or lie down, if you prefer). Close your eyes if that's more comfortable for you. Notice the feel of your body weight on the chair or on the floor. Take a deep breath in, feeling the oxygen bringing energy into your body; as you exhale, notice how it helps you relax. Notice how your feet feel on the floor—the weight, pressure, vibration, heat. Notice the back of your legs against the chair or floor, and any pressure or pulsing you feel, whether your legs feel heavy or light. Notice your back against the floor or chair. Bring your attention to your stomach—if it's tense or tight, let it soften. Take a deep breath. Notice your hands, and whether they feel tense or tight. Allow them to soften. Notice your arms, and let your shoulders be soft and relaxed; notice your neck and throat and allow them to be soft, too. Notice your jaw and let your face be soft. Notice your whole body present; take another deep breath. When you are ready, open your eyes.

▶ **Keep it up.**

"Mindfulness is a practice—and in the brain, practice makes things more permanent," says Miles. "Instead of responding to whatever gut reaction stress may bring, you can create new neural pathways that can help you respond in a more positive way." It may take some time to naturally occur, but eventually, instead of always feeling stressed when there's something amiss, you can follow a controlled, relaxed approach that will help you stay more in the moment, she says.

Find some space in your home where you can just be in the moment.

5-MINUTE YOGA STRESS-BUSTER

Increase relaxation and boost mindfulness with these four yoga poses

Mindfulness comes in many forms, but one of the easiest to try—especially when you're feeling anxious—is yoga. "Yoga is a wonderful way to help reduce stress because it links the mind and the body through the breath," explains Kristin McGee, a yoga practitioner and author of *Chair Yoga*. Many yoga poses involve breathing deeply and slowly, which calms the parasympathetic nervous system and takes the body out of fight-or-flight mode, adds McGee. Try these poses the next time your stress levels start to rise.

▶ CHILD'S POSE

Begin on your hands and knees, breathing evenly. Spread your knees wide apart, keeping big toes together, and rest your butt on your heels. Exhaling, bow forward, lowering torso to thighs and resting forehead on the floor. Keep arms extended forward on the floor, palms down. Inhale, reaching forward with arms on the floor as you continue to press back on your heels. Remain in this position for 5 to 10 deep breaths, breathing evenly and releasing all the tension in your shoulders, neck and arms.

▶ HAPPY BABY POSE

Lie faceup with knees close to chest. Reach your arms through the inside of your knees and hold the outer edge of each foot in each hand. Without letting go, press heels toward ceiling; it can help to bring your legs a bit wider as you press up. Stay here, breathing evenly for 5 to 10 breaths.

▶ SEATED FORWARD FOLD

Sit on floor (it can help to sit on a folded blanket or towel under your butt), leg straight in front of you. Hinge forward from hips and slowly lower torso toward legs, reaching hands to grasp outside of feet, ankles or shins. To deepen the stretch, use your arms to pull closer to legs. Stay here, breathing evenly for 5 to 8 breaths.

▶ SUPPORTED BRIDGE

Lie faceup on floor with knees bent, feet flat and in line with hips. Lift your hips toward the ceiling and place a yoga block under your pelvis at a comfortable height. Stay here, breathing evenly for 5 to 8 breaths. When you're ready, lift hips a little higher, remove block and lower hips to floor.

Just a few minutes
of yoga can help
calm your mind.

Spending time in nature can reduce stress hormones while also causing inflammation levels in the body to drop.

HOW NATURE HELPS US HEAL

FROM ENJOYING SCENIC PANORAMAS TO THE SCENT OF A FLOWER, TUNING IN TO THE NATURAL WORLD CAN HAVE A STRONG THERAPEUTIC EFFECT.

Even looking at
images of nature
can create calm.

Where's your happy place? For me, it's a long stretch of white sand where I can wiggle my toes while hearing the waves lap the shore as my kids splash through the low surf. Or maybe it's walking in the woods while my dog happily blazes the trail ahead, finding the occasional stream to dip her paws in.

Many of us feel this deep connection with the outdoors, and for good reason. Research shows there's a restorative quality in nature and a direct cognitive benefit from being outside. A 2015 study in the journal *Landscape and Urban Planning* found participants who walked in nature had lower levels of anxiety and rumination and improved working memory performance than those who walked in an urban setting. And a study from the University of Essex found that subjects with mental health problems who took weekly walks in the countryside had improvements in self-esteem and mood that rivaled those of antidepressants. Plus, a study from the *Journal of Environmental Psychology* found individuals who spent 40 minutes walking at a nature preserve after completing a difficult mental task reported feeling more positivity and less anger than those who walked for a similar length of time in an urban setting or who quietly read magazines while listening to music.

There's even a growing movement that advocates for spending more time in nature as a way to boost our mental and physical health. Called ecotherapy, it's based on the idea that people are connected to and impacted by the natural environment, says Linda Buzzell, a psychotherapist trained in ecotherapy in Santa Barbara, California.

You don't have to move to the mountains to reap the benefits of nature. Just a few minutes of being outdoors—better yet, being active outdoors, like taking a brisk walk through a park—can boost mood and fight stress. Can't get outside at all? There's even evidence that looking at pictures of nature can reduce stress and boost mood.

Some think nature strikes a chord because it takes us back to our roots. "There's a huge sense of joy that happens when we immerse ourselves in nature, something deeply spiritual that reminds us where we came from," says Buzzell. "Our natural instincts just perk up."

Scientists also speculate that there are very real health benefits associated with awe—something you're likely to have experienced if you've ever caught a beautiful sunset or gazed up at a towering waterfall. Even watching nature videos can induce this sense of awe.

Yet there's no one-size-fits-all prescription for how you may best benefit from interacting with nature. "Some people might enjoy a hike; others might want to spend time with animals or garden. It's all what resonates with you," says Buzzell.

No matter what you choose, pay attention to what you are experiencing. Notice the colors of the foliage in the trees around you or observe how many different types of animals you can spot along your way. If you're hiking, let your weight come fully into each step before you take the next one and find a few moments to stop along the way and enjoy the experience. Take a few minutes to focus on your breathing, whether your eyes are open or closed. Wherever you are, feel your body in space and take time to be aware of what's around you. "Just open yourself up to what you are experiencing," says Buzzell. "It doesn't have to take a lot of time to have an effect—even a small amount can have a huge impact.

TAKE A (FOREST) BATH

Forest bathing is a practice begun in Japan in the early 1980s. Called Shinrin-yoku by the Japanese Ministry of Agriculture, Forestry and Fisheries, the term literally translates as "taking in the forest atmosphere" and refers to immersing yourself in a natural setting where you can absorb the sights, sounds and smells as a way to improve your mental health. Unlike a hike, which is typically all about reaching a specific definition, forest bathing focuses on slowing down and appreciating what's around you as you move.

It seems to be working: A 2010 study of Shinrin-yoku found those who took part in forest bathing had lower levels of cortisol and lower blood pressure and heart rate compared to those who walked through an urban setting. Other research shows Shinrin-yoku may help to boost immune function, increasing white blood cells that help fight infection and other immune-system markers.

To try it on your own, think more about wandering aimlessly (without leaving the path) than going fast, pausing from time to time to notice the nature around you, whether it's an insect fluttering about or the sound of the wind rustling the leaves. Try to find a comfortable spot to observe your surroundings. If you go with a friend, try to resist talking until the end of your walk or hike—then share your experiences together.

Need a boost to your creativity? Research shows that immersing yourself in nature can help improve problem-solving skills by as much as 50 percent.

Learn how to
rebound from
adversity and
grow stronger.

BOUNCE BACK FASTER

DON'T LET STRESSFUL SITUATIONS BRING
YOU DOWN—LEARN HOW TO PERSEVERE AND EMERGE
STRONGER THAN EVER BY PRACTICING RESILIENCE.

A life-threatening illness. An automobile accident. An addiction, a crime, a battle big or small. We all will undoubtedly face adversity in our lives. A traumatic event can throw your life into turmoil. But it's how we react to these setbacks that ultimately matters—and that's where resilience comes in.

Resilience is defined as "the process of adapting well in the face of adversity, trauma, tragedy, threats or significant sources of stress—such as family and relationship problems, serious health problems or workplace and financial stressors," according to the American Psychological Association (APA). It's all about bouncing back from tough situations, whether that's as simple as dealing with an interrupted vacation or as complex as navigating the aftermath of a terrorist attack.

"Resilience is a critical part of dealing with stress—it's your ability to bend, but not break, and to sometimes even grow from adversity," notes Steven Southwick, M.D., a professor of psychiatry at Yale University School of Medicine and the author of *Resilience: Mastering Life's Greatest Challenges*.

It's not that all stress is bad, explains Southwick. "We need stress in order to grow," he notes. But if the amount of stress becomes uncontrollable, it can become harmful: "We want to get out of our comfort zone but not be overwhelmed." That's where resilience comes in.

STANDING TALL

"More than education, more than experience, more than training, a person's level of resilience will determine who succeeds and who fails. That's true in the cancer ward, it's true in the Olympics and it's true in the boardroom," Dean Becker, the president and CEO of Adaptiv Learning Systems, once told the *Harvard Business Review*.

"Resilience is one of the main things we need to learn how to do as adults," notes GinaMarie Guarino, a licensed mental health counselor in New York. Poor resilience can turn a stressful situation into a long-term crisis, while higher resilience can boost self-esteem and self-confidence, she adds.

But resilience isn't necessarily something you're born with (although there may be some genetic component, says Southwick), and it's not like you either have it or you don't. By modifying certain behaviors, thoughts and actions, anyone can learn to snap back from adversity.

"The ability to deal with stress well can be learned through skills and habits," says Southwick. "Just like anything else, you need to practice and train." Think about professions where resilience is almost part of the job description. "Police, firefighters, military personnel—these [jobs] all require you to be physically and emotionally resilient," adds Southwick. "And to succeed in those fields, you have to be properly trained."

For example, someone who wants to be a firefighter will go through training that closely matches a real-life setting as much as possible. "They get critiqued, make adjustments and get better and better—that all helps them build up their ability and confidence, even if they are placed in a problematic situation," says Southwick.

We're not saying you need to volunteer

73%

Percentage of employees who say participating in resilience training programs improved their health at your local fire department just to build up your resilience (although local first responders could always use additional support!). Rather, by practicing behaviors and adjusting your response, you can learn to boost your resilience in a wide variety of situations.

HOW TO BE MORE RESILIENT

Expose yourself.

Stress inoculation—that act of deliberately putting yourself in a scenario or situation that is intentionally difficult or stressful, but at a level you can control—is an important step in building resilience in the long term, says Southwick. "Once you've mastered a certain level, make it a little more difficult the next time."

▶ Learn to recover.

Stanford University biologist Robert Sapolsky's acclaimed book *Why Zebras Don't Get Ulcers* raises the point that while zebras are often exposed to a huge stressor (like running for their lives from a lion), they also tend to quickly forget about this stress once they're back on safe ground. Humans, on the other hand, tend to get stuck in stressful situations and take a long time to come back to baseline, says Southwick. "We don't really know how to recover—we feel stressed 24/7." So while some stress is good, we also need to practice relieving it, whether that's through exercise, meditation or something else. "A lot of resilience is learning to regulate this stress response, rather than getting crushed by it," adds Southwick.

▶ Come to terms with your emotions.

Whether you're dealing with financial worries, work stress or the loss of a loved one, it's common—and even expected—to feel anxious, sad or frustrated. "These feelings may be uncomfortable and we may try to push them aside," says Guarino. But rather than burying them, try to embrace these feelings. "You need to allow yourself to experience these emotions or they will come back to you at some point."

▶ Find support.

A key component of resilience is having a strong support network in place. That might include friends, family members, a support group or a therapist or other trained professional who can help you manage stress and talk through some of your concerns. "When you have someone who is there to listen to you, you feel a little less hopeless and helpless," says Guarino.

Social connections also help regulate your stress response and calm you down, adds Southwick. "When we know that someone has our back, that actually helps quiet the area of the brain related to fight or flight."

▶ Figure out what you can control—and let the rest go.

In his research, Southwick has discovered that truly resilient individuals are very good at differentiating what they can (and can't) control. "If you can't control a particular stressor, it's like banging your head against the wall—you won't get anywhere," says Southwick. "You need to accept whatever the issues are that are out

of your control and focus your energy on what you can take charge of."

He points to a former American POW in Vietnam whom he interviewed when writing his book. "This soldier was placed in solitary confinement for a number of years. About a year or so into it, he felt like he was going crazy, but then one day he heard a voice that told him, 'This is your life,'" says Southwick. "He said that was the moment he realized that he was going to have to deal with the situation, and rather than taking his energy to fight it, he used it to do things he could control, like stay in good physical condition and try to remain optimistic."

▶ Think positive.
The way you interpret a situation can also be crucial to making you more resilient. "Stressful things will happen, so instead of thinking about it as a negative, consider it a challenge that can make you stronger," says Southwick. "Think: 'What can I do to take on this challenge and go out of my way to grow from it and get stronger?'"

▶ Find meaning.
Resilience can also come from having something to believe in and to be strong for. Southwick cites Nelson Mandela as an example. "Here is someone who endured 30 years of imprisonment because it stood for freedom and equality," he notes. "Having a sense of purpose can give your actions a tremendous sense of meaning." Think about why you need to bounce back from a stressful situation, whether it's to be strong for your family or because you want to be a positive example to others. Having a role model who has shown this sense of resilience can also be inspiring.

> Accept what is out of your control and focus on what you can take charge of.
> —STEVEN SOUTHWICK, M.D.

Serve it up:
Look at a
challenge as a
chance to grow.

RESILIENCE BATTLE PLAN

Thinking about how you've dealt with adversity in the past can help you navigate stressful situations today—and in the future. The APA recommends considering the following questions to determine how you can best respond to current challenges.

▶ What kinds of events have been most stressful for me?

▶ How have those events typically affected me?

▶ Have I found it helpful to think of important people in my life when I am distressed?

▶ To whom have I reached out for support in working through a traumatic or stressful experience?

▶ What have I learned about myself and my interactions with others during difficult times?

▶ Has it been helpful for me to assist someone else going through a similar experience?

▶ Have I been able to overcome obstacles—and if so, how?

▶ What has helped make me feel more hopeful about the future?

The more you worry, the worse you feel—so try to stop the cycle.

7 STRATEGIES TO REDUCE WORRYING

STOP THE ENDLESS CYCLE OF NEGATIVE
THOUGHTS AND START TO
THINK POSITIVELY BY INCORPORATING
THESE THERAPEUTIC PRACTICES.

Oftentimes anxious thoughts want to help us achieve more—so don't shut them down.

— CHLOE CARMICHAEL, PH.D.

Worrying, over-thinking and agonizing over life's abundant stressors, from job insecurity and health woes to an onslaught of tragic and terrifying news headlines can plague even the most put-together among us. Approximately 44 million adults in the U.S. struggle with an anxiety disorder, according to the Anxiety and Depression Association of America. But you don't need to meet the criteria for a diagnosis to be plagued by stress-fueled cycles of rumination (which are characterized by a repetitive and sometimes constant focus on one or more worries that can, in excess, fuel anxiety or depression). In a 2018 survey conducted by the American Psychiatric Association, 39 percent of adults polled reported feeling noticeably more anxious that year than the previous one.

While you should always reach out for professional help if your thoughts are significantly interfering with your life and well-being, here are a few techniques cognitive therapists—who help people process information that might be causing distress—recommend that can help you reduce your anxious rumination today.

1 Listen up.

"A lot of people try to shut down worrisome thoughts. But when we tell them to be quiet, they end up talking louder and we can get into this internal back-and-forth with ourselves," says cognitive behavioral therapist Chloe Carmichael, Ph.D., author of *The 10 Commandments of Dating*. Instead of trying to quash the negative thought spirals, tune in to see where they might take you.

"Oftentimes anxious thoughts want to help us achieve more," explains Carmichael. That might be everything from wanting to excel at the workplace to being the best version of yourselves in a relationship, or simply trying to achieve some other goal. Recognize these thoughts as helpful, and you're more likely to channel them toward a productive end, she adds, whether that's forming a clear plan or setting up a series of goals.

2 Take action.

Let's say you're concerned about an offhand remark a family member lobbed at you during a recent gathering. Carmichael suggests writing down your concerns about the statement to get it out of your head and onto a piece of paper. From there you can also write down what you actually can do about it—rather than getting caught in a worst-case-scenario mental spiral. Pick up the phone to call a friend and talk about what's bothering you, for instance. Another option: "Consider different types of boundaries with that person," says Carmichael, "and what those boundaries might look like." For example, consider letting this person know her behavior has caused you distress, or try reducing the amount of time you spend around her or limiting the amount of personal information you share with her.

3 Fact-check.

We all freak out from time to time. But just because we feel that the flight we're about to get on is going to crash—or that most of our coworkers secretly want us fired—doesn't mean these beliefs are true. In moments where we're convinced the worst-case scenario is about to play out, try to fact-check them, advises Sara Stanizai, a cognitive therapist and owner of Prospect Therapy in Long Beach, California. Then challenge those fears with a dose of reality.

"You may not be able to say, 'this won't happen' but you can get an idea of the likelihood," Stanizai says. Do some simple research, she suggests. For example, if you are stressed about getting on a plane because you have a fear of flying, look up the odds of getting into a plane crash (which you'll find have been estimated to range from one in 7 million to one in 90 million, with 95.7 percent of plane crash victims surviving). Or be on the lookout for instances in which your coworkers actually had your back. Immersing yourself in reality can go a long way toward keeping you from incessantly worrying.

4 Find an alternative narrative.

Challenging our anxious thoughts can also take the form of thinking up alternative explanations for why a person might be acting in a certain way or why something is happening. "When we're anxious, we jump to the worst-case scenario," says Stanizai. Let's say you are convinced your significant other is acting coolly toward you, or a friend hasn't gotten back to a text you sent hours ago so she must be mad at you. "On a good day, it's easy to think your partner is preoccupied with something else or your friend doesn't have her phone on her. But on an anxious day, you worry your partner is angry with you or your friend saw your text and rolled her eyes," says Stanizai.

Rather than jumping to the conclusion that these social connections want nothing more than to sever ties with you, or that they simply don't like you as much as you like them, Carmichael suggests trying to find five other potential explanations for why someone may be acting a certain way. "This allows your mind to focus on something else," she explains. "Oftentimes another person's behavior has nothing to do with you. In fact, assuming others are thinking so many negative things about you is a bit presumptuous."

5 Break it down.

Problems that seem insurmountable are the most anxiety-provoking, explains Carmichael, because we feel powerless to do anything about them. To combat this feeling, focus on the things you can control about the issue at hand. "Break down a problem into solvable chunks," says Carmichael. Let's say you want to lose weight. Schedule a session with a personal trainer. Stock your fridge with more vegetables. Opt for a salad at lunch three times a week instead of your usual go-to fast food. These are things you can actively change so you won't worry so much about the things you can't control.

"Stepping toward a solution, even if you do it incrementally, is a positive, self-esteem building behavior," says Carmichael. The ego boost derived from meeting smaller goals can also help fuel your motivation to pursue larger ones.

6 Routinize—and rehearse—relaxation.

Being able to quiet our mind is a skill—one we have to build, and not just in the moments where we are stressed out. Stanizai notes the importance of practicing relaxation techniques like mindfulness, progressive muscle relaxation (tensing

Practicing
relaxation
techniques
in times
of low
stress
allows
you to call
upon them
when
you need
them.

**—SARA
STANIZAI,
COGNITIVE
THERAPIST**

and releasing each part of your body from head to toe for several minutes), and deep breathing in moments of low stress so we're more familiar with the tactics when that stress ratchets up. This enables us to more readily call such skills forth—like when you're lying awake at 4 a.m., exhausted but unable to stop your mind from fretting over all the things you have to do this week. Research shows that deep breathing and progressive muscle relaxation in particular can have a favorable effect on insomnia, as do mindfulness techniques like meditation done before bed.

7 Be kind to yourself.
"When we get anxious, many of us tend to be judgmental of our thoughts and feelings and end up getting into a negative spiral of self-criticism," says Carmichael. This only serves to exacerbate the anxiety, she explains, and prevents you from channeling it toward a productive end. The next time you feel inclined to lay into yourself for feeling anxious or overthinking things, try deploying some self-compassion, stat. "Imagine saying to a loved one what you're saying to yourself in those moments," she advises, and reframe those nasty sentences accordingly. (Instead of thinking, "You are so weak for being nervous right now," try, "What you're feeling is perfectly natural, and your body is preparing to face the situation at hand.")

By normalizing the anxiety, Stanizai explains, you prevent yourself from getting even more worked up over being anxious in the first place, which only serves to make anxiety worse. As a result, you're better able to channel that anxiety toward a more productive end goal—or at least ride it out until it subsides.

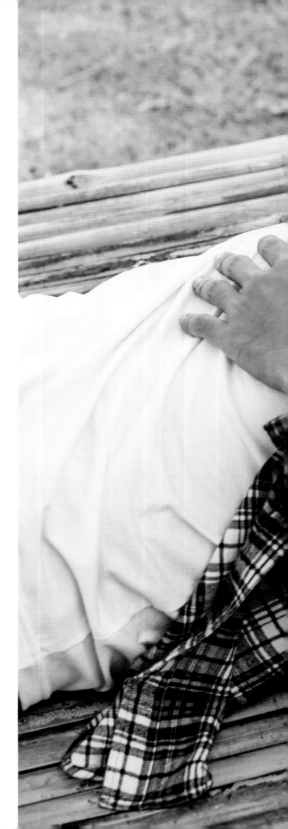

Relaxation techniques can quickly impact your outlook.

Don't spiral: A therapist can help get you back on track.

WHEN TO GET HELP

"If your anxious thoughts are getting in the way of your ability to focus at work, be present during social encounters, interfering with your sleep or romantic life, or keeping you from hobbies you once loved, it's wise to reach out to a therapist for assistance," says cognitive therapist Sara Stanizai. That's especially true if you've tried addressing your anxiety or rumination on your own and nothing seems to work. A behavioral therapist can help you learn and rehearse emotion-regulation strategies, restructure unhelpful thoughts and beliefs that give rise to troubling behaviors like rumination, and build new ways of thinking that not only reduce your worry but help you to lead a more productive, self-caring and balanced life.

Just a few
minutes of
activity can
boost mood.

SWEAT AWAY STRESS

EXERCISE REMAINS ONE OF THE BEST WAYS
TO DAMPEN ANXIETY AND LEAVE YOU FEELING
STRONGER, MORE CONFIDENT AND IN
CONTROL OF WHATEVER ELSE YOU HAVE TO FACE.

5 MINUTES

Minimum amount of time aerobic exercise takes to reduce anxiety

When her 15-year-old gives her attitude, or her small business gets overwhelming, or she's facing some other stressful situation, Sandi Simon laces up her sneakers, puts on her headphones, and heads out for a run. "It's the best way I know to release all of that built-up tension and frustration and just lose myself in the movement and the music," says the 50-year-old mom of two from New York City. "When I come back home, I always feel like I'm starting fresh."

Working out has long been considered one of the best ways to reduce stress and boost mood. Whether it's pounding out your aggressions in a kickboxing class or taking a meditative stroll through the woods, getting your body up and moving kick-starts a number of physiological and psychological changes.

"Exercise seems to alter the receptors in the brain responsible for the stress response," notes Bill Roberts, M.D., a sports medicine doctor and a past president of the American College for Sports Medicine. When you work out, stress hormones like adrenaline and cortisol start to dip, while feel-good endorphins take over.

Working out also gives the body a chance to practice dealing with stress, notes a paper published by the American Psychological Association. The authors write: "[Exercise] forces the body's physiological systems—all of which are involved in the stress response—to communicate much more closely than usual: The cardiovascular system communicates with the renal system, which communicates with the muscular system. And all of these are controlled by the central and sympathetic nervous systems, which also must communicate with each other. This workout of the body's communication system may be the true value of exercise; the more sedentary we get, the less efficient our bodies are in responding to stress."

It doesn't seem to matter what type of exercise you do—any kind of physical activity can make a difference, notes Roberts. That said, we all have our preferences for exercise (and some of us can't stand it at all). So the best type of workout to beat stress may largely come down to what you enjoy doing, adds Roberts. "Pick something you like, and do it on a regular basis," he says. By making exercise a regular part of your lifestyle, you'll not only improve your health in a number of ways, you'll be better able to handle stress when it does strike.

Not sure where to begin? Consider these activities when your stress levels start to rise.

WHEN YOU'RE FEELING FRUSTRATED
High-intensity interval training

Boss got you crazy? Moody teen setting you on edge? Ready to pound the dashboard of your car after yet another traffic jam? You may want to try HIIT. Short for High-Intensity Interval Training, these workouts mix bursts of high-intensity activity with lower-intensity rest periods, so you're able to recover and start again.

"A high-intensity workout is a great way to blow off steam and release feel-good endorphins," notes Rob Arthur, a trainer and health coach based in

Raleigh, North Carolina. This type of high-energy movement provides near-immediate stress release and can be an effective way to reduce stress quickly, he adds. If you're someone with a lot of chronic stress issues, though, you may want to try a different form of exercise, says Arthur. "In the long run, our bodies only have so much capacity for stress, so if you're throwing a physical stressor like a high-intensity workout onto an emotional stressor, like your job, it may ultimately end up depleting you."

TRY THIS High-intensity workouts can vary, depending on what you like to do. Try sprint intervals outside or on the treadmill, boot camp, kickboxing, rowing intervals or anything else that will jack up your heart rate for anywhere from 10 seconds to two minutes, then take equal or more time to recover. Repeat this sequence at least one or two more times. Since the activities tend to be intense, check with your doctor before starting any of these workouts.

WHEN EVERYTHING FEELS OVERWHELMING
Meditative movements

When your to-do list is a mile long or you've got so much to do that you don't even know where to begin, that's the time when a slower-paced movement can help. "Lower-key activities can still have a strong effect on stress," notes Arthur. "When you do slow, deliberate movements such as yoga, tai chi or qigong, it shifts your body from the fight-or-flight sympathetic nervous system to the more relaxed parasympathetic system, which works to reduce stress levels."

Studies show that slow, meditative exercises like qigong and tai chi can create physiological changes that help diminish stress. One randomized control study found that just 10 minutes of a qigong class helped reduce cortisol levels, anxiety and negative mood, while boosting levels of natural killer immune cells compared to a placebo group. Other studies have found that after being exposed to a form of stress, those who practiced qigong showed significantly lower signs of stress hormones. "Combining a slower, deep breathing with movement helps induce a sense of calm and feelings of relaxation," adds Martin Esen, 86, founder of Mantis Kung Fu Qigong and Tai Chi in Cherry Hill, New Jersey, who has been practicing the martial art for almost 70 years. "There's a whole mind-body-breath coordination taking place that creates a significant change in how you feel," he adds.

TRY THIS Sample a tai chi or qigong class, or give a relaxing yoga class a try. Even meditative walking—making a deliberate effort to be aware of both your breath and your movements—can help foster this sense of calm and control.

WHEN YOU NEED TO FOCUS
Instructive activities

Big project or assignment requiring all of your attention? Doing a workout that forces you to dial in to what you are doing can also help you get away from your worries and build the discipline and concentration you need to get the job done. "Often our stress comes from worrying about what we have to do," says Arthur. "When you perform a task that requires you to really focus on the activity, it takes you away from that concern about the future and makes you more fully present." That means when it's time to get the job done, you're ready and able to go, he adds.

Activities that require you to think also force you to take a "time-out" from your problems, notes a review published in *Frontiers in Psychiatry*. Exercise as a distraction seems to have a longer-lasting effect on anxiety than other therapies meant to take you away from your worries.

TRY THIS Any activity that requires hand-eye coordination, whether it's hitting a tennis ball or jumping rope, can help heighten this focus. Even workouts where you have to pay careful attention to your movements, such as strength training or doing Pilates, require a sense of awareness.

WHEN YOU'RE FEELING ISOLATED
Team activities

Stress can come from social isolation, especially if you're going through a tough time or just looking to make some new friends. Sports have long been a community-builder, whether that's your local softball rec league or volleyball team. More into individual endeavors? Local clubs also do weekly or monthly get-togethers in a noncompetitive atmosphere. Plus, you'll not only get the stress relief from exercise, you'll also build your social network and make new connections.

TRY THIS Sign up with a recreational sports league in your area, or look for local cycling, running or walking clubs that offer weekly get-togethers to train and socialize.

Being active with friends increases the stress relief.

Source: American Psychological
Association

The meditative movement of swimming can be soothing.

Use your time
off the grid
to connect
with nature.

6 WAYS TO A DIGITAL DETOX

READY TO STEP AWAY FROM TECHNOLOGY?
IT'S EASIER THAN YOU THINK—HERE'S
HOW TO UNPLUG WITHOUT GOING NUTS.

ALERT YOUR INNER CIRCLE

Turning off your phones and computer can make it difficult for someone to reach you in an emergency—or just get your mom worried when she can't get in touch. So alert friends and family that you're going off–line for a few hours, a day, or however long you plan to be out of touch. Same idea goes for your job, if your boss is someone who likes to get in touch outside normal working hours. Or just post on your social media that you're having a #digitaldetox— your followers will understand.

Give some
warning
before you
turn things off.

HAVE A PLAN

Choose a time that's realistic for you and think about what you want to accomplish in your break from technology. Even if it's just reading a book, drawing, baking cookies or organizing your space, know what you want to do so that you aren't tempted to seek out your tech.

Head out to stock up on things you need for the hobbies you love.

Look Ma, no screens! Time outdoors can offer new perspective.

EASE BACK IN SLOWLY

You might be overwhelmed by a barrage of emails and messages if you've spent any significant time off–line. Use your time away to have some perspective on what's really important and what can wait. You don't have to answer every message or email right away. Prioritize what you can, and don't sweat the small stuff.

Whatever the
season, soak in
your surroundings.

GET OUTSIDE

Embrace Mother Nature: Take a walk in the park (or go for a day hike), play with your kids, watch the sunset. This is a good time to practice some mindfulness, like how the breeze feels on your skin or what sounds the leaves make when you walk over them.

Download a playlist that makes you feel happy.

DON'T GO COLD TURKEY

You can use technology for some good, like playing music while you read or cook. You don't even have to go the full 24 hours—just pick a few hours at night or on a weekend day and see how that makes you feel.

📱 EXPECT SOME ANXIETY

"You do get some phantom pains when you don't have your phone with you," says Tanya Schevitz, spokesperson for the unplugging advocacy group Reboot, who admits to experiencing separation anxiety for the first few hours of unplugging. "It can feel a little uncomfortable in the beginning but in a way you'll feel freed from not having to respond to your phone every time it buzzes or pings."

When it's time to plug back in, remember how it felt to be disconnected.

The author relishes her time away from screens.

MY UNPLUGGING EXPERIMENT

AN EDITOR AND WRITER FINDS SHE CAN BETTER
TAP HER CREATIVE SIDE WHEN SHE
TAKES REGULAR BREAKS FROM TECHNOLOGY.

ne weekend day a month, for the full day or a half day, I unplug for a digital detox. My phone, computer and smartwatch are turned off and tucked away. When I wake up, I look out my window into my backyard and wonder what the day has in store instead of picking up my phone first thing.

I feel calmer because I'm not obligated to check my email or social feeds and retweet, repost, share and repeat. I can do my own thing—finally.

The first time I tried this, it was an auspicious New Year's day, when I only took out my phone once to take a picture in a yoga studio to document the moment. Maybe because it was the first attempt and it was the fresh start to the year, but it somehow seemed easier than other, later tries.

Over the months that followed, I had my struggles at walking away from technology, even if only for a few hours. In April, I only managed a half day and every hour of it felt...forced (which it was), and constricting (which it was, but only in my head). I was distracted during several morning meditation attempts and just wanted to "get on with it." But a breakthrough came for me when I had a change of scenery: A long walk outside turned into stopping by a community garden and spontaneously starting to sketch the scenery while others gardened— definitely not something I normally do! It was a lovely turn of events for my unplugged brain. But the moment it hit five hours, I was ready to power on.

Looking back, that single five-hour stretch taught me a lot about contentment, my constant reliance on sounds and textual engagement from my phone, and what it means to be the keeper of my own state of mind.

Back inside, I embrace my creativity: I pull out my sketch pad and draw, or find my journal and blurt out grand ideas that I've been keeping bottled up. Or I'll put on the record player for an impromptu dance session in my living room. By day's end I've usually read from a great book, painted, napped, journaled, watched the sunset and eaten well as the vinyl spins away.

Like with any detox, I work to actively treat myself better than I would when I am on autopilot. I feed myself something delicious at every meal and take the time to do some batch-cooking of meals so that I'm set up for the week ahead with healthy foods. I sit down for long enough to drink a full cup of tea and do nothing else until I'm done (no multitasking!). On digital detox days, everything I do seems more special. Fresh air and a stroll set a good tone and tell my brain that something is different about today. I'll also try to walk more mindfully while I'm out, slowing down to take in my surroundings more deeply and noticing the sights, sounds, and smells. I make sure to pay attention to my breathing as I walk.

These days are for daydreaming, crafting, forgiving myself, breathing and letting my natural impulses take me by the hand to see where they lead me. And though it sometimes feels incredibly tough to follow through, every time I take a digital detox day, it leaves a lasting impression on me about just how crafty and inquisitive I am, all on my own. And the more days I take off from technology, the more naturally curious and patient I am in my everyday life. And the better I am to myself, the better I can be to the world around me.

—Cat Perry

With scenery like this there's no need for WiFi.

"The more I take time away from technology, the more naturally curious I am in my life."

Knitting's meditative aspect yields many benefits.

HOBBY TIME

CAN YOUR FAVORITE LEISURE-TIME ACTIVITY HELP BUST STRESS? RESEARCH SAYS IT CAN DO THAT—AND MORE. HERE'S WHY WE SHOULD ALL SCHEDULE A LITTLE MORE DOWN TIME.

When Beth Gannon starts to feel stressed, she picks up her needles and begins to knit. Whether it's coming out of a board meeting that makes her temper rise or waiting for an important phone call about a loved one's surgery, time and again she's found that the repetitive, soothing aspect of knitting starts to calm her down and helps her feel less anxious or upset.

"Knitting helps distract me from second-guessing my actions and gives me something productive to do that gets my blood pressure back under control," says the 52-year-old attorney from New York City. "Plus, I use really good wool—so having something that feels really soft like cashmere offers a tactile sensation that in itself is inherently relaxing."

Having a healthy hobby can be enormously helpful at coping with stress, experts say. And there's really no limits to what your activity needs to be. From meditative actions like knitting or pottery to social experiences like joining a hiking club or taking a cooking class, hobbies are a way to take your mind off daily challenges and give you some time to simply enjoy yourself. And that's something most of us just don't do enough of, says GinaMarie Guarino, a licensed mental health counselor in New York.

"It's so important to just set aside time for yourself that doesn't have anything to do with work or other obligations," explains Guarino. "Too often we get so caught up in our day-to-day responsibilities that we don't give ourselves a break and relax."

Hobbies can be social or individual, active or quiet—but they all have the common thread of allowing you to focus on yourself by doing something you enjoy. "Someone who is more extroverted and needs social interaction might like a group activity to help recharge, while someone else might be much happier doing a crossword puzzle or reading a good book," says Guarino. "It just depends on what you like to do."

RESEARCHING RELAXATION

A wide variety of studies show that having a hobby can provide numerous benefits to both your body and mind, and can be an effective way to reduce chronic stress. "In general, research has shown that a hobby can help you cope with work-related stress by providing a different kind of challenge, allowing you to disengage from whatever task you were facing," explains Guarino. "It can also help to manage your time better, so you actually become more efficient."

Here's what other studies have shown occurs when it comes to keeping up a healthy hobby.

▶ **It helps to clear your mind.**
British researcher Betsan Corkhill, author of *Knit for Health and Wellness*, has done numerous studies on the therapeutic benefits of knitting, and discovered that the bilateral, rhythmic motion can create a relaxing, almost meditative state. "When you're deeply concentrating on a difficult stitch or project, it demands all of your focus and attention, but if you choose an easy project, you can enter a near-flow state that can help get you in a state of daydreaming—all of which are beneficial when you're stuck thinking about a problem or a stressful event," says Corkhill.

Hobbies are a way to take your mind off daily challenges and enjoy yourself.

—GINAMARIE GUARINO, MENTAL HEALTH COUNSELOR

Activities like baking provide a distraction from problems.

> **Anyone can benefit from a hobby if they give it a try.**
>
> —RESEARCHER BETSAN CORKHILL

▶ **It protects your brain.**

Researchers from the University of Pittsburgh School of Medicine have found engaging in hobbies for an hour or more a day may help protect against dementia later in life, compared to those who did hobbies for fewer than 30 minutes a day.

▶ **It makes you happier.**

A study published in *Psychosomatic Medicine* showed that when subjects took part in activities that were classified as enjoyable leisure time (like hobbies), they had lower blood pressure levels and lower total levels of the stress hormone cortisol. They also had lower levels of depression, as well as lower physical characteristics like body mass index and waist circumference. And a study by Corkhill found that 81 percent of respondents who knit three or more times a week reported feeling better during and after knitting; 54 percent said they felt at least happy or very happy.

▶ **It keeps your heart healthier.**

A 2015 study from India showed that subjects who enjoyed doing hobbies on a regular basis had better coronary blood flow compared to those who did not take part in any structured leisure-time activities. The researchers concluded that in the early stages of arteriosclerosis, having a hobby may improve cardiovascular function.

▶ **It may help you live longer.**

A 2016 study found regularly engaging in hobbies helped to extend longevity among a group of elderly Japanese people. It also helped provide more life purpose and reduce the decline in quality of life.

FIND YOUR PERFECT ESCAPE

Not quite sure what activity to pick up in your spare time? The possibilities are almost limitless, says Rachel Dubrow, a therapist based in Northfield, Illinois. Take a workout class, join a book club, take up quilting—or get a membership to visit your local botanical garden or zoo. "It doesn't have to be mind-blowing," she notes. "It can be something simple that you just enjoy doing and which gives you some time for yourself." Still stuck? Check out these hobby favorites based on overall activity.

▶ **If you like being active**

We know exercise is a great way to put a damper on stress, which means activities like running, cycling, swimming or shooting hoops can help improve your health while clearing your mind. Choose something high-energy, like training for a 5K, or more meditative, like tai chi or yoga. Either way, you'll work your muscles while boosting your mood.

▶ **If you're a social butterfly**

Can't wait to connect with others? Consider a hobby that keeps you involved with a group, whether that's joining a team or taking part in a local choral group. Research has established the importance of maintaining social connections for improved health and well-being. Even better, join a group that gives back. "Volunteer to be involved with womething bigger than just yourself," says Guarino. "When you feel like you are an active member of a helpful cause, it not only helps others, it also improves your own self-esteem."

▶ If you are a good student

There are ample opportunities to explore adult education programs at local colleges and universities, or check out online classes at websites like Massive Open Online Courses (*mooc.org*), which offers programs in everything from aerospace engineering to anatomy from more than 100 institutions, including Harvard, MIT and the University of California, Berkeley. "It doesn't have to involve a long commitment—just explore what you are interested in," says Guarino.

▶ If you are crafty

Enjoy making things from scratch? Crafty hobbies like knitting, sewing, scrapbooking and quilting allow you to focus on a specific task without letting distractions get in the way. Knitting, for example, involves coordinated movements that engage the brain and create a more meditative, relaxed state, according to the website stitchlinks.com.

▶ If you love nature

Gardening, hiking or beachcombing all bring you up close and personal with the great outdoors—which in and of itself has been shown to relieve stress and anxiety. Find a local patch of greenery or community garden, or create your own window-box garden if you don't have access to land you can use.

Spending time
with your pooch
makes both of you
feel happier.

THE HEALING POWER OF PETS

WHETHER YOU'RE COZYING UP TO YOUR CAT,
PETTING YOUR POOCH OR JUST GAZING AT A COLORFUL
AQUARIUM, THERE'S NO BETTER NATURAL
STRESS RELIEVER THAN SPENDING TIME WITH ANIMALS.

8%

Percentage of U.S. companies that allow dogs at work— ideally to improve job satisfaction and reduce stress.

There is almost no stressful situation in our home that our dog Trixie can't fix. When my kids are angry at us, or fighting with each other, or feeling they have way too much to do, a few minutes of snuggle time against her soft black-and-white fur makes them feel better. When my husband gets aggravated about work, giving her a belly rub helps his own tension dissipate. And when I wake up feeling like I'm facing a mountain of responsibilities, a walk to the park followed by some play time at the dog run suddenly makes everything seem much more doable.

Trixie may not be able to solve all of our problems, but I can say with certainty that being around that wagging tail makes everyone a little bit happier. I'm not sure if it's the way she looks at us with her soulful brown eyes or the way she plops down next to us when she thinks we're feeling blue. I just know that spending time with her is a surefire way to relieve stress.

I'm not the only one to feel this way. Numerous research studies show that having a pet—and spending time around animals in general—is one of the most effective ways to improve mood, fight loneliness, reduce anxiety and depression and manage stress. And there are numerous other health benefits to having a pet as well.

"Having a positive relationship with animals is something that goes back thousands of years," notes Steven Feldman, executive director of the Human Animal Bond Research Institute (HABRI), an organization that helps to fund research about the relationship between humans and animals. "Our brains are hardwired to observe and connect with other creatures."

PART OF THE FAMILY

Pets have carved a very big place in most homes today, with 65 percent of U.S. households keeping some kind of animal companion. Americans are expected to spend more than $72 billion this year on their animals, according to research from the American Pet Products Association. And pets aren't just living in our homes: A 2015 Harris poll found 95 percent of pet owners consider their animals a member of their family.

It's no surprise, then, that our brains have similar responses to our pets as we do with our kids. Human-animal interactions have been known to increase levels of oxytocin in the brain—the same neurochemical that promotes maternal care in mammals. Oxytocin is also associated with slowing heart rate and breathing, quieting blood pressure and reducing stress hormones, while creating a sense of calm, comfort and focus. It's also a two-way street: Studies have shown that oxytocin levels are increased in dogs when they interact with their owners compared to when they spend time with strangers.

In addition to oxytocin, other neurological changes are also triggered when animals and humans get to hang out. Dopamine—the neurochemical associated with pleasure—and feel-good endorphins are also shown to increase when the two-legged and four-legged subjects spend time together, while the stress hormones cortisol, epinephrine and norepinephrine all decline. "Research has shown that when you are petting a dog, the dog is

Having a furry friend can help you live longer.

experiencing the same stress relief that you get," says Feldman.

Animals can also help reduce stress by keeping your mind off your problems, says Alan Beck, Sc.D., director of the Center of Human-Animal Bond at Purdue University. "Much like mindfulness, being with your pet is a way of keeping you in the present—you're not bemoaning the past or worrying about the future. Animals naturally lend themselves to holding your attention."

There are other physical and psychological benefits as well. "We've seen evidence where talking to an animal reduces blood pressure to lower levels than you'd get when you are simply at rest," says Beck. Several studies have shown that dog owners have lower blood pressure levels than those who don't keep a canine in the house, although researchers aren't sure whether that's because having a pooch produces a calming effect, or if it's because you're naturally more active by having to walk a dog a few times a day. (A study in the journal *BMC Public Health* found dog owners walk on average 22 minutes more per day than people who do not have a dog, which brings its own stress-reducing benefits.)

Having an animal at home may also boost heart health. The American Heart Association issued a statement a few years ago that concluded pet ownership—particularly having canine companions—may be an effective way to help reduce your risk of cardiovascular disease. Studies have also shown that dog owners appear to have lower cholesterol and triglyceride levels than non-owners, even after accounting for variables like diet, smoking and body mass index.

There are advantages for mental health as well. A survey by HABRI found that 74 percent of pet owners reported having a pet helped improve mental health. "Numerous studies have shown that rates of depression can be reduced with animals," says Feldman. And a recent study published last year in *BMC Psychiatry* reported that pets are an effective way to help manage long-term mental health problems. "We've gone from thinking that it's nice to have a pet to realizing it may prove to be an essential way of coping with some mental health issues," adds Feldman.

NOT JUST FOR THE DOGS

Although much of the research about the power of pets has been conducted around canines, you don't have to be a dog person to experience the positive benefit of being around animals. One study from the University of Minnesota's Stroke Institute found that owning a cat helped to reduce an owner's risk of a heart attack by nearly one-third. And a study published in the *Journal of Vascular and Interventional Neurology* found that people who never owned a cat were about 40 percent more likely to die after having a heart attack than those who had a cat in the house.

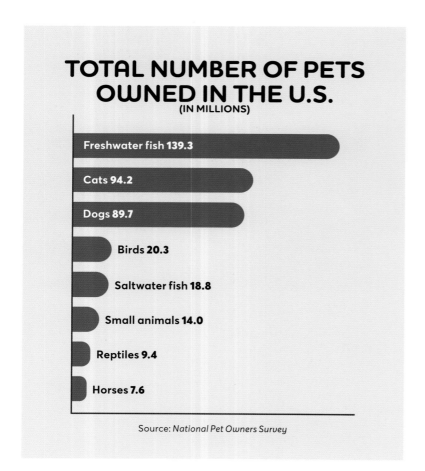

TOTAL NUMBER OF PETS OWNED IN THE U.S.
(IN MILLIONS)

Freshwater fish **139.3**

Cats **94.2**

Dogs **89.7**

Birds **20.3**

Saltwater fish **18.8**

Small animals **14.0**

Reptiles **9.4**

Horses **7.6**

Source: *National Pet Owners Survey*

Cats can be just as affectionate as dogs.

Interacting with
your pet boosts
feel-good
hormones.

More into scaly creatures? "There is a large and dedicated subset of pet owners who have a strong affinity for reptiles and who love their bearded dragons and snakes as much as someone else might love their dog," notes Feldman. You'll get much of the same social connectivity with having a pet boa or tortoise as you might with a cat or dog, he adds, either from communicating with other owners or from spending time with your own animal companion. (Plus, for those with allergies, there's no fur, dander or hair to worry about.)

Even having fish can produce its own benefits—especially when it comes to mental health. Research has shown that after looking at aquariums, people reported being in a better mood and had lower heart rates and blood pressure levels. One of Beck's studies found that subjects who spent 20 minutes looking at a fish tank before undergoing dental surgery had significantly lower rates of stress during surgery than a control group, and the same low levels as those who had undergone hypnosis. The benefits can extend to cognitive issues, as well—another of Beck's studies found that when patients with Alzheimer's disease dined in front of aquariums filled with brightly hued fish, they ate better and needed less nutritional supplementation; they were also more attentive and less lethargic.

Pets may not provide all of the answers when it comes to reducing stress, but for those who appreciate having an animal at home, it's an easy way to feel better fast when tension levels start to rise. "We're told to eat your veggies and exercise because those are both part of being healthy," says Feldman. "In our opinion, having a pet also belongs on that list."

Or maybe you're a big fan of horses? Saddle up, because some of the most well-researched health benefits come from interacting with equines. A study among British horse riders found that more than 80 percent said they felt extremely cheerful, relaxed, happy or active after they went riding. Equine-assisted therapy has been used for several generations as a therapeutic approach for both physical and mental health concerns, including depression, post-traumatic stress disorder and anxiety. You don't even have to climb on: Many equine therapy programs simply involve grooming the horse or interacting in other ways.

ANIMALS ON DEMAND

Not allowed to own a pet, or just not around enough to take care of one? Get your animal fix in with these strategies.

▶ VOLUNTEER AT A SHELTER

Most animal shelters, like the ASPCA, have volunteer opportunities, whether taking regular dog-walking shifts or playing with the animals. Some centers even need volunteers to just sit and read or play music to help acclimate the animals to human presence.

▶ GO TO THE ZOO

The animals may be behind glass or a moat, but you can still find animal companionship at your local zoo. A study from the St. Louis Zoo found visitors were happier, more energized and less tense after they spent some time interacting with a stingray exhibit.

▶ WATCH SOME YOUTUBE

Or whatever other cute cat video you come across. "We're coded to find watching animals comforting, so even a few minutes of looking at animals interacting reduces feelings of stress," notes Alan Beck, director of Purdue University's Center of Human-Animal Bond.

▶ TAKE UP BIRD-WATCHING

Grab some binoculars and find some peace and quiet. You'll get some fresh air and have time to reflect on what's around you.

Even a day at the zoo makes you feel better.

1 PHONE A FRIEND.

A heart-to-heart with a pal can be just what you need to feel more at ease. "Things always feel less hopeless when you are able to talk them out with someone who understands," says GinaMarie Guarino, a licensed mental health counselor in New York. "You feel better able to take on whatever challenge you face." Research backs her point: A 2007 review article in the journal *Psychiatry* found social support can go a long way toward improving mental health and fighting stress by increasing resilience and reducing risky behaviors.

People with strong social support are more resilient.

22 STRESS-BUSTING STRATEGIES

TRY THESE QUICK AND EASY TIPS
WHEN YOU START TO FEEL ANXIOUS,
UNEASY OR OVERWHELMED.

2
HOLD SOMETHING COLD.

Freaking out? Grab an ice cube or a cold drink. Feeling something cold in your hand immediately forces you into the present moment and distracts you from whatever is causing you stress, advises Guarino.

3 Help someone else.
Volunteering for a worthy cause—whether that's getting groceries for your elderly neighbor or walking some dogs at a local animal rescue shelter—can provide a good deal of help in making you feel better about whatever else is stressing you out. "Doing good helps you feel good," notes Guarino. Research has also shown that volunteering helps people feel more socially connected and may even improve physical outcomes, like preventing high blood pressure, according to a study published in the journal *Psychology and Aging*.

4 Take a deep breath.
To stop stress fast, just breathe in and out slowly. "Bringing oxygen into your body creates a calming sensation and pushes your body from its heightened state of alert into something more soothing," says Guarino. Try this simple exercise: Inhale deeply for four counts through your nose, filling up your belly with air. Hold this breath for seven counts; then exhale for eight counts through your mouth. "Focusing on the rhythm and counting forces you to be fully present," she adds.

5 Listen to your favorite tunes.
Whether you've chosen an upbeat pop playlist or a soothing symphony, research shows that listening to music can have a clear effect on your well-being. Studies show that mellow music, in particular, can help lower blood pressure and heart rate and reduce anxiety. Nature sounds (crashing waves, chirping birds, rustling wind) can also help. And an inspirational jam can also go a long way toward helping you out of a funk. A 2013 review from McGill University found that listening to music not only reduced levels of the stress hormone cortisol, it also helped improve immune function.

6 Hit the museum.
Take your mind off whatever ails you by surrounding yourself with visual beauty. Whether you've picked a modern sculpture garden or a classic portrait gallery, spending even a short amount of time immersed in a museum or gallery can help visually transport you away from whatever is causing you stress, notes Guarino.

7 Take a walk.
Even just a quick stroll outside can be enough to reduce anxiety. A 2010 British study found that within five minutes of walking outside, subjects reported an increase in self-esteem and mood. Other research has shown that exercising in natural environments is associated with a decrease in tension, confusion, anger and depression, and an increase in energy levels.

8 Write down what you're grateful for.
Take a few moments to jot down everything that makes you grateful, from close friends and family to your ability to get out and enjoy the sunshine. When you can remember what makes you feel grateful, it often cancels out negative thoughts and concerns. To keep a positive attitude, write frequently—the more you maintain a journal, the more you tend to notice the things you appreciate around you, experts say.

9 SNEAK IN A QUICK SNOOZE.

Stress can interfere with your ability to get a good night's sleep, but the opposite is also true—when you are well rested, you're better able to cope with stressful situations. Regular sleep helps improve concentration, regulate mood and lower overall stress. When you don't get enough sleep, you're not only cranky, you're also more likelier to overreact and turn seemingly small situations into major causes of stress: A 2014 study from the University of California, Berkeley found that a lack of sleep makes you more emotionally reactive, more impulsive and more sensitive to negative stimuli.

10 Have a good laugh.
Whether it's watching a few minutes of "Funny or Die" on YouTube or your favorite silly movie on Netflix, humor is one of the best ways to make you feel better, fast. "It's important to make time for laughter," notes Rachel Dubrow, LCSW, a therapist based in Chicago. Laughing has also been shown to reduce cortisol levels while increasing endorphin production.

11 Take a Buzzfeed quiz.
Sure, you don't really need to know which kind of Disney Princess you best identify with, but that's not the point. "Websites like this are perfect for stress management because they take your mind off whatever's worrying you, even if it's just for a few minutes," notes Dubrow. So go ahead: Find out how many kids you'll have based on your favorite Pop-Tarts flavor. We won't judge.

12 Do something new.
Whether you find a crafting class at the local community center or a yoga routine in the park, get out of your funk and into a new environment, advises Dubrow. "Do something you've never done before—you'll challenge yourself in a new way and distract yourself from what might be worrying you."

13 Put your PJs in the dryer.
Then take them out and put them on. Ah—instant stress relief, notes Susan Albers, Psy.D., a psychologist at the Cleveland Clinic and the author of *50 Ways to Soothe Yourself Without Food.*

"Anything like this that feels good and changes your senses can quickly make you feel better."

14 Buy yourself a bouquet.
Fresh flowers not only look (and smell) great—they can also be just the sensory distraction you need to boost your mood and take your mind off stress. A study from Harvard Medical School found people reported being more compassionate toward others, had less worry and anxiety and were less depressed when fresh-cut flowers were present in their homes. Keep some plants or flowers at your desk for when work seems overwhelming, or place a vase full of flowers front and center in your home.

15 Do some self-massage.
A soothing rubdown can relieve tight muscles and adhesions that can come when you feel stressed. Can't get to a masseuse? DIY: Place a warm heating pad or cloth around your neck and shoulders for about 10 minutes, keeping your eyes closed and trying to relax. When you're done, stand near a wall and place a lacrosse or tennis ball behind your back. Then lean into the ball and gently roll it a few inches in each direction to help massage away tightness and tension in your muscles.

16 Squeeze a stress ball.
There's a reason those soft balls feel so good to scrunch. Research has shown that stress toys like these can help relieve patients' anxiety before or during

35% Percentage of us who sleep fewer than seven hours a night— a stress trigger

surgery; another study found stress balls helped sixth-graders be less distracted during class. Minor distractions like these can also help to boost productivity at work and make it easier to pay attention to whatever you're doing—so you're less likely to allow stress to take over.

18 Take some magnesium.

"Magnesium is known as the antistress mineral," says Carolyn Dean, M.D., N.D., author of *The Complete Natural Medicine Guide to Women's Health*. "If you are feeling stressed or anxious, take an absorbable form of magnesium, such as a magnesium citrate powder mixed with water and lemon." Serotonin, the feel-good brain chemical, depends on magnesium for its production and function, she adds. "A person who is going through a stressful period without sufficient magnesium can set up a deficit that, if not corrected, can linger, causing depression, unhappiness and further health problems." You can also find magnesium in a variety of whole foods, including dark leafy-green vegetables such as kale, spinach, Swiss chard, as well as in organic nuts and seeds such as pecans, almonds, cashews and pumpkin seeds.

19 Tidy up.

All that clutter around your desk, in your kitchen or just taking up space wherever you're spending time can also make it more difficult to relax and unwind. And when you're at the office, a messy work space can make your to-do list seem even more endless. Spend a few minutes throwing out what you don't need and put away what's not immediately important. You'll not only be more efficient, you'll also be a little less anxious.

20 Brew a cup of tea.

A warm mug of tea is more than just soothing—it's also a stress-buster. A wide variety of herbal teas have a long history of helping to relieve anxiety and induce calm. Long-popular choices include peppermint (which can also help relax tense muscles), chamomile (a proven sleep aid), and passionflower (which has long been used by herbalists to combat anxiety). If you prefer some caffeine, try green tea, which is also loaded with antioxidants as well as theanine, an amino acid that has a calming effect.

21 Get busy in bed.

With the right circumstances, sex is a perfect way to relieve both stress and tension. The caveat is that you need to feel comfortable with your partner and the situation, but when the timing is right, the immediacy of getting it on and the rush of endorphins that comes with climaxing means there's very little room in your brain to worry about anything else.

22 SMELL SOMETHING RELAXING.

Aromatherapy is one of the best ways to find instant calm. Light a candle, use a diffuser or rub on some lotion or a few drops of an essential oil. Key scents that can help increase relaxation and reduce tension include lavender, bergamot, jasmine, ylang ylang and chamomile.

SPECIAL THANKS TO CONTRIBUTING WRITERS:

Anna Davies, Cat Perry, Andrea Pyros, Brittany Risher, Katherine Schreiber, Layla Shaffer and Celia Shatzman

CENTENNIAL BOOKS

An Imprint of
Centennial Media, LLC
40 Worth St., 10th Floor
New York, NY 10013, U.S.A.

ISBN 978-1-951274-12-2
Distributed by
Simon & Schuster, Inc.
1230 Avenue of the Americas
New York, NY 10020, U.S.A.

For information about custom editions, special sales, and premium and corporate purchases,
please contact Centennial Media at contact@centennialmedia.com.

Manufactured in China

Publishers & Co-Founders Ben Harris, Sebastian Raatz
Editorial Director Annabel Vered
Creative Director Jessica Power
Executive Editor Janet Giovanelli
Design Director Ben Margherita
Senior Art Director Laurene Chavez
Art Directors Natali Suasnavas, Joseph Ulatowski
Production Manager Paul Rodina
Production Assistant Alyssa Swiderski
Editorial Assistant Tiana Schippa